MODERN BIG DATA ARCHITECTURES

Founded in 1807, John Wiley & Sons is the oldest independent publishing company in the United States. With offices in North America, Europe, Asia, and Australia, Wiley is globally committed to developing and marketing print and electronic products and services for our customers' professional and personal knowledge and understanding.

The Wiley CIO series provides information, tools, and insights to IT executives and managers. The products in this series cover a wide range of topics that supply strategic and implementation guidance on the latest technology trends, leadership, and emerging best practices.

MODERN BIG DATA ARCHITECTURES

A MULTI-AGENT SYSTEMS PERSPECTIVE

Dominik Ryżko

WILEY

For general information on our other products and services or for technical support, please contact our Customer Care Department within the United States at (800) 762-2974, outside the United States at (317) 572-3993, or fax (317) 572-4002.

Wiley publishes in a variety of print and electronic formats and by print-on-demand. Some material included with standard print versions of this book may not be included in e-books or in print-on-demand. If this book refers to media such as a CD or DVD that is not included in the version you purchased, you may download this material at http://booksupport.wiley.com. For more information about Wiley products, visit www.wiley.com.

Library of Congress Cataloging-in-Publication Data is Available:

ISBN 978-1-119-59784-1 (hardback)
ISBN 978-1-119-59794-0 (ePDF)
ISBN 978-1-119-59793-3 (ePub)

Cover Design: Wiley
Cover Image: © Pobytov/Getty Images

Printed in the United States of America

V46841C25-1032-4809-AF40-454C5F126241_030320

CONTENTS

LIST OF FIGURES

LIST OF TABLES

PREFACE

Over several years of my career in IT, I have observed how various ideas and technologies have come and gone, taking different paths, from being new and innovative to maturity and adoption, only to be replaced by even newer concepts as they arrive. Some gained popularity very quickly and became the buzzwords of their time, something that everybody tries and claims to be doing. Such is the case of *big data*, the popularity of which skyrocketed and was embraced by research, industry, and governments alike. In 2012 the Obama Administration announced the Big Data Research and Development Initiative [2012] acknowledging it as a key enabler to *accelerate the pace of discovery in science and engineering, strengthen our national security, and transform teaching and learning*. Only recently has big data been overshadowed by the widespread adoption of artificial intelligence (AI), which by the way, builds on the foundations of big data. However, big data will remain strong for the foreseeable future.

Other promising technologies from the past have not stood the test of time. The rise of statistical approaches to AI, and deep learning in particular in the past decade, gave the final blow to the symbolic methods, which I found elegant and fascinated me at the time of my undergraduate studies in the 1990s. Have the logical systems passed forever? Possibly not; after all, there are still open questions as on how humans analyze facts, reason, and make decisions, which we are not yet able to model purely by statistical methods. Only the future will show us in which direction science will progress.

Another interesting story is related to Multi-Agent Systems (MAS), the field I picked for my PhD and later research. While the concept of an agent, or closely related actor, go way back to the 1970s, it never gained wide popularity outside the relatively narrow research community and some niche business applications. Despite bringing in innovative views on information system paradigms and promises of solving some of its challenges, the idea never became widely adopted.

As my focus started to switch toward industry projects and I became more and more involved with building large scale big data and AI systems, I observed that some of the fundamental assumptions behind MAS have made their way into mainstream information systems. Monolith systems, dominant at the beginning of my career, started giving way to services and later to micro-services. Physical devices distributed in the physical environment gained computational power and thus built-in intelligence and increased autonomy. These changes were happening not because MAS were gaining in popularity, but due to the fact that it made sense to solve real issues in this way.

Finally, a few years back, I was able to formulate a more concrete conclusion, which can be used as a working thesis for this book – *mainstream computer science is on a convergence path with multi-agent paradigms*. Or to be more specific: *the fundamental building blocks of modern information systems have been gaining the properties of those attributed to agents in MAS and thus the whole system has become more adaptive, autonomous, and intelligent.* I decided to devote some time to studying these analogies, by comparing the fundamental assumptions and paradigms as well as by looking at the applications of MAS in solving various problems in the big data area. This book summarizes this research by taking a journey through modern big data architectures viewed through the eyes of the MAS domain.

I hope the view taken in this book will be fresh and interesting and will inspire further critical thinking about the evolution of contemporary information systems and the direction they are heading.

Dominik Ryżko
Warsaw
August 2019

ACKNOWLEDGMENTS

As the work on this book from the initial idea to its completion stretches over a period of a few years, it is not possible to mention all the people with whom I have discussed the ideas and the book itself during this period. However, a few of them have had significantly more influence on my thoughts and the final shape of the work.

Most of all I want to thank my family for supporting me and accepting the effort and time needed for such endeavor. I want to thank my supervisors and directors at the Institute of Computer Science, Warsaw University of Technology, Professors Marzena Kryszkiewicz, Henryk Rybiński, Mieczysław Muraszkiewicz, and Jarosław Arabas for encouraging me to pick up this project and coming up with valuable advice. Special thanks go to my friend and colleague Bartłomiej Trwardowski with whom I have spent numerous hours exchanging thoughts and ideas on various scientific topics and who was kind enough to provide feedback on an early draft. Last by not least I thank my past and future students, who are among the main recipients of this work. Your open and curious minds were a big motivator to make this book insightful, covering the most important ideas but also focusing on practical topics. I hope you will find it this way.

ACRONYMS

ACID	Atomicity, Consistency, Independence, Durability
ACL	Asynchronous Connection-Less
AI	Artificial Intelligence
AMI	Advanced Metering Infrastructure
API	Application Programming Interface
BASE	Basically Available, Soft state, Eventually consistent
BDI	Belief Desire Intention
BI	Business Intelligence
BPEL	Business Process Execution Language
CAP	Consistency, Availability, Partitioning
CEP	Complex Event Processing
CPS	Cyber-Physical Systems
CRM	Customer Relationship Management
CSO	Cooperative Smart Object
CUDA	Compute Unified Device Architecture
DAG	Directed Acyclic Graph
DBMS	DataBase Management System
DFS	Distributed File System
DL	Description Logic
DMP	Data Management Platform
DNS	Domain Name System
DSN	Distributed Sensor Networks
DSP	Demand-Side Platform
EDA	Event-Driven Architecture
EHR	Electronic Health Records
ERP	Enterprise Resource Planning
ESB	Enterprise Service Bus
ETL	Extract Transform Load
FAP	Femto-Access Points
GIS	Geographical Information Systems
GPGPU	General Purpose computing on Graphics Processing Units
GPS	Global Positioning System
HDFS	Hadoop Distributed File System
HEP	High Energy Physics
IaaS	Infrastructure as a Service
IDS	Intrusion Detection Systems
IFP	Information Flow Processing

JSON	JavaScript Object Notation
KPI	Key Performance Indicator
LHC	Large Hadron Collider
MAS	Multi-Agent System
MCC	Mobile Cloud Computing
MEC	Mobile Edge Computing
ML	Machine Learning
MRI	Magnetic Resonance Imaging
M2M	Machine to Machine
NFC	Near-Field Communication
NLP	Natural Language Processing
OWL	Web Ontology Language
OS	Operating System
PaaS	Platform as a Service
PCA	Principal Component Analysis
PET	Positron Emission Tomography
PSL	Probabilistic Soft Logic
QoS	Quality of Service
RDF	Resource Description Framework
REST	Representational State TRansfer
RFID	Radio Frequency IDentification
RPC	Remote Procedure Call
RTB	Real-Time Bidding
SaaS	Software as a Service
SEM	Search Engine Marketing
SEO	Search Engine Optimization
SGD	Stochastic Gradient Descent
SLA	Service Level Agreement
SOA	Service Oriented Architecture
SPARQL	Simple Protocol and RDF Query Language
SRL	Statistical Relational Learning
SQL	Structured Query Language
SSP	Supply-Side Platform
URI	Uniform Resource Identifier
VM	Virtual Machine
VPN	Virtual Private Network
WSN	Wireless Sensor Networks
XML	eXtensible Markup Language

CHAPTER 1

Introduction

1.1 Motivation

In recent years, *big data* has emerged as one of the leading trends not only in computer science, but due to its potential, also in economy, science, and major branches of the industry. People realized that huge data sets have become a key asset which should be taken into account in evaluating business opportunities, company valuations, or product development. Several major mergers and acquisitions in recent years have been driven not only in order to gain synergies, customer base, or market access, but also to obtain access to valuable customer data. For example, Microsoft's acquisition of Linkedin gave it data on jobs, skills, career paths, and a contact network of millions of workers across the globe.

For technology vendors, consultancies as well as numerous startups, this rapid growth opened up huge new business opportunities. According to IDC, the market value of big data and business analytics is expected to grow beyond $200 Billion by the year 2020. Forbes [2017]. These forecasts have fueled huge investments in big data related research and development efforts, both in academia and in industry, leading to a wide range of proposed architectures, solutions, models, algorithms, as well as commercial products.

Large industry players have made the big data concept fundamental to their products, architectures, and strategies. Every day, new ventures emerge which concentrate solely on big data as an opportunity for innovation and growth. Those who failed to follow the trend early see the rising competition and disruption, even in well established and heavily regulated industries such as banking or insurance, as can be observed by the growing number of *fintech* and *insurtech* ventures.

Academia has been intensively updating curricula to educate the next generation of data scientists, big data engineers, DevOps, etc. The research areas and goals of computer science departments have followed suit. New dedicated MOOCs (Massive Online Open Courses) become available every month and gather thousands of attendants. The number of conference tracks and entirely new events around the subjects of analytics and processing of big data is growing rapidly each year.

While there is no single agreed on definition of *big data*, it is commonly regarded as a general move towards analytics and applications, which rely heavily on processing of extremely large data sets in order to provide intelligent, personalized services to the users and other services in the ecosystem. This trend has been largely supported by recent advances in parallel computing architectures, emergence of NoSQL databases, cloud computing technologies and continuous improvements in machine learning and other branches of Artificial Intelligence (AI).

Multi-Agent Systems (MAS) use the concept of the *agent* as a central entity for building systems. This is often confusing as the term is heavily overloaded even within computer science, not to mention its use in multiple other disciplines such as economy, sociology, cognitive science, etc. MAS however iterates specifically the properties an agent should implement. It should be autonomous, understood as making its own decision based on internal state, goals, and observations. An agent should be proactive, so it should act when it believes it is appropriate not only when explicitly called. Finally, it should be intelligent in the AI sense of intelligence, therefore capable of solving complex tasks and learning by past experiences. Building on such components, MAS tries to assemble complex systems in which agents communicate asynchronously and collaboratively solve given tasks.

Even though MAS emerged as a separate field of research much earlier than big data, it failed to achieve such wide adoption and popularity. We can identify several reasons for this. One is that, until recently, there were no advanced and mature architectures for efficient distributed asynchronous processing. Only in the last decade the limitations to Moore's Law increased the efforts towards parallel computations. Another reason is the radical approach to the distribution of control in MAS. Agents were proposed as highly independent, autonomous, proactive entities communicating with the use of "soft" protocols, e.g. negotiation, argumentation etc. These assumptions were not in line with available means for monitoring of such systems, and so were unacceptable for several practical industry applications, where strict control and risk minimization are key, e.g. energy grid management, financial systems, traffic monitoring, etc.

This publication argues that the fields of big data and MAS have a lot in common. If we track the evolution of the IT systems from monolith, through SOA to microservices and most recently cyber-physical systems, we can see that the elementary system components more and more resemble agents as proposed many decades back. We rely more and more on loosely-coupled components centered around some well defined functionality and capable of autonomous and flexible operations even if other components fail or are temporarily out of reach. Now that distributed, cloud based computing has become standard, database paradigms have shifted from a strict transactional approach and physical objects obtain built-in intelligence, MAS approach no longer looks radical and unfeasible.

It seems we have arrived at the point where several research results achieved in both fields can be combined and benefit from cross-fertilization of ideas, tools, and architectures. Mobile agents for sensor networks can be applied for real time analytics in the fast growing area of the Internet of Things (IoT). Distributed machine learning algorithms can be coordinated with multi-agent cooperation protocols. Mobile and IoT cloud computing environments experience challenges related to resources and latency similar to the ones present in MAS especially for mobile agents.

On the other hand, modern big data environments offer unprecedented possibilities of performing large scale computations both in batch and streaming mode, which can greatly enhance capabilities of MAS. Cloud resources supporting mobile and IoT devices might well be used to empower intelligent agents located in the environment. On the lower level, modern distributed programming libraries (e.g. Scala Akka) can greatly improve performance of MAS, which often use less advanced environments, not capable of efficient thread and resource management.

1.2   Assumptions

While establishing the scope and focus of this book, several assumptions and compromises had to be made. Firstly, when describing a field such as Big Data, where new concepts and projects emerge on a daily basis, it is difficult to resist the temptation to include every new finding, so the book will be as up to date as possible at the time of publishing. On the other hand it is difficult to predict the future of freshly proposed solutions, before they become more mature and are hardened by real life applications.

Therefore, difficult choices have been made and some might argue that a particular important architecture, project, or framework has been left out. In general, I have been following the rule of writing about topics, which have some proven maturity, e.g. have become mainstream Apache projects, have been followed by highly cited publications, have been applied by at least one of the large and recognized industry players, etc.

Secondly, since the book title refers to big data architectures, the contents concentrate on large scale solutions capable of solving practical problems experienced in the industry. Therefore, specific tools applicable at particular points in the larger architectures are described only to the point where they are relevant from the point of view of the big picture they take part in, rather than in their internal and technical details. For example Hadoop, which is often regarded as a technological synonym for big data, is described as a component for batch processing used in larger big data architectures. Map-Reduce, Hadoops', underlying algorithm, is presented as one of the generic computational models for processing extremely large data sets. Similarly, Spark is an example of stream processing and plays that role in larger big data setups.

In the field of MAS things have been somewhat easier, since the field is more mature in general and several comprehensive textbooks have been published to date, which summarize the research and development efforts in this area. Therefore, major agent models and architectures are described in line with the state of the art long established in the field. This is complemented with some more recent and more specific examples of applications of multi-agent paradigms in solving various big data problems.

1.3   For Whom Is This Book?

This book could be of interest to both researchers and practitioners from the fields of big data, analytics, machine learning, MAS, distributed computing, cloud computing, distributed artificial intelligence, as well as a number of other related fields.

The intention has been, for anyone from the fields mentioned above to see the current state of the art in distributed, asynchronous processing of massive data sets. As well as this it will be shown how various field and areas of research relate to each other by tackling similar issues and challenges from their respective perspectives.

For big data practitioners not familiar with MAS research it may come as a surprise how many relevant ideas and concepts have already been analyzed several years back. MAS researchers will find several big data environments, libraries, and tools very useful for taking their systems to the next level of efficiency.

In the end I hope that this book will initiate mutual discussion and exchange of ideas, which is to some extent already present but could become much more intense and fruitful.

1.4   Book Structure

The book is organized as follows. Chapter 2 discusses how major paradigms and concepts have changed over the last few decades, leading to the current landscape. Specifically we will analyze how the evolution of IT architectures influenced storage and analytics of the data. We will also look at the shift of paradigms in database systems, the growing role of the cloud, the Internet, and the IoT. Also the concepts of an agent and an actor are introduced. We conclude by discussing how all these trends led to the rise of big data.

In Chapter 3 we look at where the data comes from in the big data setups. We start with the Internet as the most commonly available data source today. Then we iterate over various branches of science and industry looking at how much data they generate and what is specific about each of them. Finally, the IoT as the fast growing source of huge data streams is described.

Once we are familiar with the data sources, the book dives into specific tasks which need to be performed with the use of the data. Chapter 4 looks at the most important challenges that research and industry is working on in the big data area. This covers recommender systems, search, real time bidding, as well as multiple other topics.

Cloud computing is discussed in Chapter 5. It deserves a separate chapter as a major trend shaping the creation of the next generation of information systems. We look at the advantages and challenges of utilizing cloud resources and how it enables the building of scalable, distributed big data systems. The means for efficient cloud management both in VM and container based setups are described.

In Chapter 6 several big data architectures are presented. We start with fundamental computational models and move towards more complex setups. This includes among others Lambda and Kappa architectures, which have recently emerged as important design patterns for building scalable big data processing and analytics. A separate section is devoted to stream processing.

The means for data analytics and building machine learning models are the subject of Chapter 7. The role of SQL versus other forms of ad-hoc interaction with the data is analyzed. Tools and architectures for providing SQL capabilities in noSQL environments are analyzed. We look at frameworks and tools for efficient building, deploying, and testing of machine learning models.

Geographically distributed systems are the topic of Chapter 8. We will take a look at how the latest trends driven by mobile computing and the IoT led to the emergence of edge and fog computing as new paradigms for extending the cloud towards the distributed elements of the cyber-physical systems.

The work is closed by Chapter 9 with a summary and conclusions. References to the literature complete the volume.

CHAPTER 2

Evolution of IT Architectures and Paradigms

2.1 Evolution of IT Architectures

Over recent decades corporate IT architectures have evolved significantly. Starting from the large monolith application, through the introduction of web services and the emergence of the Service Oriented Architecture (SOA), which has evolved into microservices, we went through the wide adoption of cloud computing and have now reached the popularity of edge computing, the Internet of Things and cyber-physical systems. Each of these steps required a change in the way we produced, processed, stored, and analyzed the data, which will be explored in the subsequent sections of this chapter.

2.1.1 Monolith

Back in the 1990s corporate systems were built mainly as large monolith applications. They were based on a number of tightly coupled modules with strong interdependencies. This caused high development and maintenance costs. At the beginning of the software development process it is beneficial to have all the building blocks in one place, but as the system grows, it becomes tedious to track all the internal dependencies and the code base becomes hard to manage. The growing size and complexity of a monolith impacts all software life cycle steps influencing design, development, testing, and deployment.

Each design and development decision taken in a monolith system has long lasting consequences. This phenomenon is well described by the term technical debt coined by Cunningham Cunningham [1993]. The larger the system, the more reluctant we are to introduce necessary changes and the debt grows.

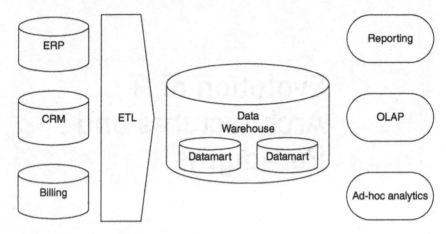

Figure 2.1   BI in monolith architecture.

In monolith systems scalability is limited. More instances of the system can be set up to introduce load balancing. However, replicating the entire functionality each time is very costly. Demand for different functionalities can vary, and we do not have the tools to scale them separately.

On the other hand it is relatively easy to manage and analyze the data processed by such systems. We usually have a single underlying database with a relational schema, which can be easily exported to an analytical environment, typically a data warehouse, where a set of BI tools produce reports, KPI visuals, dashboards, etc. In the worst case we have to deal with a handful of monolith systems (e.g. ERP, CRM, Billing, etc.) and introduce some form of Extract Transform Load (ETL) processing, in order to combine them before loading into the warehouse. Figure 2.1 shows the overall reporting architecture in the world of monolith systems.

The methodology for creating and maintaining a data warehouse is well researched by now. Typically, the following layers can be identified in such a system:

- Data Source Layer – systems and sources which feed the data into the warehouse
- Data Extraction Layer – responsible for pulling the data into the warehouse
- Staging Area – the area where data stays before the major transformations (ETL) begins
- ETL Layer – in this layer is a set of processes which transform the data into the format usable for reporting and analysis

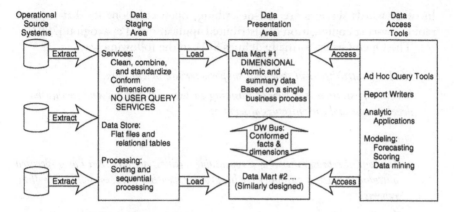

Figure 2.2 Data warehouse architecture.
Source: Kimball and Ross (2011). Reproduced with permission.

- Data Storage Layer – stores the data after it has been transformed and cleaned
- Data Logic Layer – gives semantic to the data by defining the report structure
- Data Presentation Layer – provides interface to the user
- Metadata Layer – describes the data stored in the warehouse
- System Operations Layer – allows administrators to manage the data warehouse

In large organizations data marts are usually created, which are sub-sets of the overall data limited and optimized for specific groups of users. The Data Marts are efficient for analysis across multiple predefined dimensions such as time, region, product, etc. Kimball and Ross [2011]. A Data warehouse architecture is shown in Figure 2.2.

While ETL processes in a large organization can become quite complex, entities coming from a single monolith system are well structured and related with each other. What remains, is managing the relations between the data sets from various monoliths and from external sources if we wish to include them in our reporting setup.

2.1.2 Service Oriented Architecture

In the 2000s Service Oriented Architecture (SOA) paradigms were introduced. The idea was to break the large systems into reusable components, implementing specific groups of functionalities accessible by strictly defined APIs. In SOA the services are more loosely coupled then in the monolith systems.

In other words services are self-describing, open components that support rapid, low-cost composition of distributed applications. Papazoglou [2003].

The Open Group formally defines SOA in the following way:

SOA is an architectural style that supports service-orientation.

Service-orientation is a way of thinking in terms of services and service-based development and the outcomes of services.

A service:

- *Is a logical representation of a repeatable business activity that has a specified outcome (e.g. check customer credit, provide weather data, consolidate drilling reports)*
- *Is self-contained*
- *May be composed of other services*
- *Is a "black box" to consumers of the service*

Such a setup requires a composition layer, which provides coordination, monitoring, conformance, and QoS functionalities in order to provide composite services to the clients. The backbone of the SOA system which allows it to do this is called the Enterprise Service Bus (ESB). The following specific tasks can be handled by the ESB. Josuttis [2007]:

- Providing connectivity
- Data transformation
- (Intelligent) routing
- Dealing with security
- Dealing with reliability
- Service management
- Monitoring and logging

In order to manage the business processes, specific languages, e.g. XML-based BPEL (Business Process Execution Language) and business process servers have been introduced. The services can be built in various technologies as long as their APIs follow Web Service standards.

As the number of services and potential interactions in SOA increase, new problems arise. The dynamic nature of collaborating services means several issues can be experienced at run-time. Network can lag, messages can be lost, services can experience performance problems or crash entirely.

Therefore, monitoring of such systems becomes a crucial task. Administrators need to be able to pinpoint quickly where the source of the business process failure lies. Obviously any information which can help to anticipate potential problems in SOA, before they arise and have a big impact, is of great value.

From the perspective of this book, it is interesting to mention applications of Multi-Agent Systems to solve the issues described above. For example Ryzko and Ihnatowicz [2011] propose to distribute intelligent agents throughout the SOA system, which are tasked with monitoring selected services and following process execution. Whenever a certain service becomes unavailable or predefined KPIs (e.g. service queue length, response time, etc.) cross predefined threshold, alerts are raised. This early warning system provides the opportunity to take action before a substantial breach of the overall system SLAs takes place.

The central idea of SOA is to put emphasis on the good definition of the service interfaces and to hide the underlying logic and data. This imposes problems if we want to analyze data in a traditional way, as with the monolith systems, i.e. plugging each service into an ETL framework and integrating it into a BI solution.

If we do not want to violate the SOA principles we can pull the data from the services with the use of existing data contracts. If done regularly, this would allow us to obtain the complete history of required information. However, this model is not synchronized with the real pace in which the data is produced and can impose delays and efficiency problems.

A way to deal with the problems described above is to use a push model. This approach is called Event-Driven Architecture (EDA). The services publish events, which can be collected as they appear by subscribed entities. This reduces the network load, since data is published once rather than being requested several times as in a pull model.

In the book *SOA Patterns* by Rotem-Gal-Oz et al. [2012] an aggregated reporting pattern for SOA is described. The pattern is designed to overcome the distribution of data across services by creating a service that gathers immutable copies of data from multiple services for reporting purposes. The service works as follows. Firstly, the data is transferred from the source services into the raw data store. Then it is processed by the transformation backend and put into the reporting store, usually containing joined and aggregated data. Finally, an SQL output endpoint is provided in order to plug in ad-hoc SQL and reporting tools.

Four different ways of getting the data into the aggregated reporting are proposed:

- Actively calling other services – use of other services contracts to get new data
- Passively getting data from services – subscribing to batch data exports or events

- Service SQL push – services export a view of internal data
- ETL SQL push – as in the option above but with the involvement of external ETL tool

The advantages of using aggregated reporting include: holding of immutable data with possible versioning if changes are received, providing single SQL interface for reporting, possibility to highly optimize reporting efficiency. As for the disadvantages, examples are: high complexity of the solution, relatively large latency in data access, and duplication of data.

2.1.3 Microservices

Most recently, the microservice architecture has gained significant attention. This paradigm calls for the creation of a large number, even larger than in SOA, of small, independent, highly decoupled processes communicating via APIs. Newman [2015].

Microservices should be small and focused on performing one specific piece of functionality. There is no strict definition of small, however typically we mean that it can be developed and maintained by a single team in a relatively short period of time. The natural boundary prohibits creation of tight links with other services and motivates concentration on designing efficient API. In most situations, REST (Representational State Transfer) is a good integration method between microservices. It has a low complexity when compared to other protocols and allows for fast prototyping and development.

Another key property of microservices is their independence. Often the word autonomy is used here. However, since autonomy is a property of Agents, which will be used in this text in a different context, the term independence will be used. By this we mean that each microservice can be deployed separately and is communicating only with the use of the network calls to APIs. If we need to change something in the implementation, this should be invisible to end users as long as we stick to the agreed API contract.

To some extent microservice architecture can be regarded as an evolution of SOA. However, some of the properties and functionalities, which are attributed to SOA architecture are addressed differently. Firstly, SOA advises the use of an Enterprise Service Bus in order to facilitate communication between the services. Microservices typically use lightweight mesh message passing, for example based on exchange of JSON (JavaScript Object Notation) or Protobuf (Protocol Buffer) files via REST APIs. In the more complex microservice environments it is beneficial to introduce additional publish-subscribe mechanisms (e.g. Kafka) which do not necessarily provide centralized monitoring and SLA management, but are able to process a very larger number of messages. In other words, routing logic has been moved from the pipelines into the services, which decide where to send notifications and how to respond to them.

Secondly, the microservice architecture streamlines the deployment process, by introducing fast, automatic, continuous integration supported by dedicated continuous integration tools. Finally, microservices pushed forward the widespread adoption of noSQL databases. While SOA introduced local storage related to particular services, and thus was able to apply the first non-relational storages, in microservice architecture an even wider variety of database models is used, with a significant representation of NoSQL databases (see Section 2.3).

One of the main advantages of the microservice architecture is the ability to build systems in a more flexible and agile way. We can use different technologies, which are best suited to particular functionalities. Obviously, from the perspective of a development department it is not desirable to introduce too many technologies into a company, but within some predefined borders this flexibility brings clear benefits.

Systems composed of microservices can be built to be more resilient. When one service fails it does not have to pull everything else down. If all microservices implement some sort of fallback for such situations, then the entire system will degrade gracefully, providing some subset of the functionalities, which can still be operational.

Also the system scalability can be more flexible with microservices. The number of running instances can be adjusted at a single microservice level. With the current cloud technologies this can be done dynamically on the runtime (see Section 2.4).

Obviously there are also challenges, which come with the use of the microservice architecture. With the growing number of independent components, the number of interdependencies is also growing and becomes more difficult to track. Each dependency results in the need to think about error handling, failover, and SLA. Various clients of a microservice can have different needs, resulting in a multitude of API versions. A common way of solving this is by using API gateways, which provide a single interface to a particular application.

Tracking of transactions is even more challenging than in SOA, where there were some possibilities of doing it on the process logic level. In Microservice architecture there is no such centralized mechanism. In some cases the only possibility is to introduce a compensation mechanism, which triggers a sequence of messages with the goal of canceling the effect of a previously performed API calls.

Independent evolution of microservices and their APIs can result in problems with incompatible object schemas. This can be mitigated to some extent by introducing schema versioning via shared libraries.

Testing and monitoring of systems based on microservice architecture is another complex task. As a foolproof testing method for such systems is not feasible, microservices have motivated a whole new range of approaches. One example is chaos testing, which is based on the assumption that anything can fail at any time. Therefore, random services are made unavailable in order to see the effect of such scenarios on the system at large. Each service which does not demonstrate sufficiently good failover, needs to be improved.

Such a testing approach has to be coupled with efficient monitoring and recovery. As microservice architecture relies heavily on APIs, monitoring of API health is key. If API becomes unavailable or its response time degrades, it is the first sign of a system moving towards failure. Also most relevant KPIs should be monitored both on the technical (e.g. endpoint response time) and business level (e.g. average client transaction time). In the most complex cases logging services can be of great help. By processing or reviewing service logs manually, engineers can discover undesired behavior patterns and introduce suitable improvement to prevent them in the future.

2.1.3.1 Microservice data analytics

In order to perform any analytics or big data processing in the microservice architecture we have to collect the data. In the easiest scenario, there is a shared database, where a number of services store their data. Then we have only one place to pull the data from. However, this integration method can cause several problems. Firstly, it requires all the consumers to adapt to the changes in the schema. Secondly, a single database model needs to be used for all the services. Thirdly, the logic responsible for managing the single data object can be located in several different places, which makes it hard to maintain.

In a fully implemented microservice architecture, with local data stores kept by particular services, challenges similar to the ones experienced in the SOA architecture will arise. For small amounts of information, a call to the APIs can get us the data we need. However, this will not work for large volumes, since it can impact the performance of the services. Even if we implement additional batch APIs, it still drains the resources of a service, which has to handle regular API calls while performing work resulting from regular transactions.

A step further would be to implement dedicated data pumps, which push the data from a service database to the analytics or reporting storage. They can be scheduled to run in the time of low service usage, in order to limit the impact on the performance.

Finally, an event based publish-subscribe mechanism can be used. In this approach an event is emitted each time the data in the service is changed. Such events are pushed to the publish-subscribe mechanism, e.g. Kafka.

From there events are pulled by interested parties or finally stored in some long term storage, e.g. Hadoop.

This approach has several advantages including:

1. Low impact on the service performance – we just perform additional operation on the data which the service works on anyway.
2. Availability of the data changes in real time – events appear just after a particular piece of data has been changed.
3. Possibility to store long history of data changes – if we store all the events we can recreate history of the changes to the particular data structures.

On the downside:

1. Each event has to be handled in order to make suitable changes to the target data store (e.g. update a particular value).
2. Mechanisms such as Kafka work in "eventually consistent" state, which means at any particular time we cannot assume we have seen all of the events published in the entire system, nor can we assume we will receive them in the same order they were generated in. This means, if we need a complete data set some compensation methods which can access the service database might still be needed.

2.2 Actors and Agents

In this section we look at the differences and similarities between the *agent* and *actor* models. Agents and actors are terms that emerged from different fields and, while they can be used to tackle similar problems, there are some differences between the two concepts. Agent is a fundamental concept in the Multi-Agent Systems field, while the concept of actors emerged from the discipline of Distributed Computing and is now widely used in modern frameworks such as *Akka*, commonly applied to implement the real time processing of data in several big data architectures.

2.2.1 Actors

The concept of an actor is quite old and was originally coined by Hewitt et al. [1973]. It has been developed as a formal mathematical model for distributed computations. Actors are typically used for organizing coarse-grained lock-free non-deterministic concurrency.

The fundamental properties describing an actor are persistence, internal state, and asynchronous communication. This means, that the internal state of an actor can never be directly accessed from the outside. Actors are passive between processing of messages. When a message is received an *Actor* can:

- send a finite number of messages to other actors
- create a finite number of new actors
- select the behavior to be used when it receives the next message

Messaging is handled directly between the actors using the underlying protocol. It is assumed that each message will be delivered at most once. However, there is no guarantee on the time of delivery and it is possible for the message to never reach the destination. This also influences the order of the messages, which does not have to be kept.

Apart from messages not being delivered, actors themselves can fail. In order to tackle this, the actor model provides supervision. It is a relation between the actors in which a supervisor delegates tasks to subordinates and then monitors their work and responds to failures if they arise. For example in the Akka actor implementation the following four possibilities are identified:

- Resume the subordinate, keeping its accumulated internal state
- Restart the subordinate, clearing out its accumulated internal state
- Stop the subordinate permanently
- Escalate the failure, thereby failing itself

The last option indicates that there can be more levels of supervision in the system. Indeed, the actor model allows for a tree of monitoring aggregating all the actors under one top-level "Root Actor" (see Figure 2.3).

Because we allow actors to be restarted or entirely killed, there are mechanisms in the actor model supporting seamless operation of the system despite such events. First of all, addresses do not change when actors are restarted, so when the agent is recreated the messages can be sent in the same way as before. Furthermore, mailboxes persist independently from the actors, so even if an actor is killed, the unprocessed messages are not lost.

Due to advances in the hardware architectures supporting parallel computation, interest in industrial applications of the actor model has risen significantly. Several of the modern programming languages provide actor model implementations, e.g. Erlang (built-in support), Akka (Scala), CAF (C++), Pulsar (Python), Actix (Rust). While these implementation vary in the details, the underlying assumptions are based on the original actor abstraction.

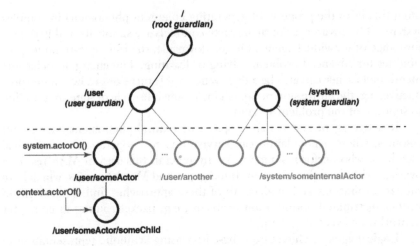

Figure 2.3   Akka actor hierarchy.
Source: Light Bend. Part 1: Actor Architecture. Reproduced from https://doc.akka.io/ docs/akka/current/guide/tutorial_1.html. Licensed under https://www.apache .org/licenses/License-2.0

2.2.2   Agents

Agents are intelligent, autonomous, and proactive entities, which are continuously active. They communicate via asynchronous messages, but can also receive information indirectly from the environment which they constantly observe. For example reactive agent systems take advantage of the fact that the information can be exchanged by modification of the environment, without the need for direct exchange of messages. This makes such systems more difficult to model and design, but can be more flexible in several real life scenarios.

The agent model is more sophisticated, compared to the actor model, in the sense that it is not purely message driven, but gives possibility to balance between reactive, deliberative, and proactive behavior. With this freedom comes more ambiguity as to how to find this balance for a particular application.

The theory of multi-agent systems distinguishes a number of model architectures such as reactive architecture, logical architecture, BDI (Belief Desire Intention) architecture, and layered architectures. Weiss [1999].

The reactive agent architecture is based on a simple state-free model, which operates by using a set of predefined rules of the form *input → action*. By combined effort of several such agents and the use of the environment for exchange of information, such systems are able to perform several tasks, often thanks to the property of generating emergent phenomena in complex systems. The advantages of such reactive models are simplicity and high performance of individual agents. On the downside, the lack of state limits possibilities for advanced problem solving or learning. The emergent behaviors mentioned earlier can also be a disadvantage if it turns out to be counterproductive, e.g. the entire system can fall into some idle cycle of states not leading to solution of the problem at hand.

Reactive agent systems are inspired by natural phenomena such as ant colonies, where a population can survive due to cooperation of individual members, who perform simple tasks. In general, this area of MAS research overlaps with the fields of Swarm Intelligence and Metaheuristics, which have similar inspirations and models. All of these approaches find applications in various distributed optimization problems, e.g. packet routing in computer networks. Pedro et al. [2009].

Logical agent architecture is based on using symbolic representation in the form of logic as a formalism for knowledge modeling. This architecture uses the agent's perception to update the agent state. Actions are chosen as a result of the reasoning process. Such an approach has the advantage of using the declarative style to program agents, which is easy to understand and interpret at any given time. If we use one of the well known logical formalisms, then any existing reasoning engine can be applied. The disadvantages of logical agents are: the computational complexity of most logical systems, the problem of mapping real life problems into a set of logical formulae, the handling of temporal dependencies, incomplete or uncertain information, etc. While there are specific logics, which allow for temporal and common-sense reasoning, their complexity is even higher than that of the simple logical systems. An example of a logical system designed to handle common-sense reasoning and at the same time support distribution of knowledge among agents is Distributed Default Logic described in more detail in another work by the author of this book. Ryżko and Rybiński [2006]; Ryżko et al. [2008].

BDI agents are a type of logical agent. Rao and Georgeff [1991]. Rather than maintaining a single logical theory, like in the logical agents described above, three components of the agent's knowledge are distinguished:

- Beliefs – a model of the world
- Desires – a model of goals that the agent can achieve
- Intentions – the goals that the agent commits to

Figure 2.4 shows the internal structure of a BDI agent. The decision-making process starts with the Belief Revision Function (BFR), which takes the input from the agent sensors and transforms the model of the world into a new consistent state. Based on the current beliefs, the agent generates Desires,

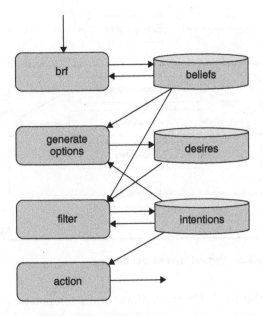

Figure 2.4   BDI architecture.

which are achievable states, which the agent would like to reach given its goals. The agent commits to a subset of desires, which become Intentions.

The advantages of BDI architecture include modularity and following common-sense decision-making processes, easy to interpret by humans. On the other hand, as a variation of a logical model, it has all of its disadvantages mentioned above.

Layered architectures can be divided into two sub-architectures, namely horizontal and vertical. Horizontal layered architectures consist of a set of modules, all of which receive the input from agent sensors and process them separately. Outputs from all of the modules are joined by a coordinating mechanism, which decides on the final action. In this approach, layers operate separately and, therefore, can use different knowledge representation formalisms. It is possible to embed such architecture models described above, i.e. reactive or logical models. By combining them in one architecture one can take advantage of their advantages in specific situations. E.g. if a quick decision is needed, a reactive layer can be applied. Whereas, if a more complex plan is needed, logical architecture or a dedicated planning engine can be used. An example of a horizontally layered agent model is shown in Figure 2.5.

In a vertical layered architecture the input is received by one module only, which after processing passes the result to the next level and so on. The final

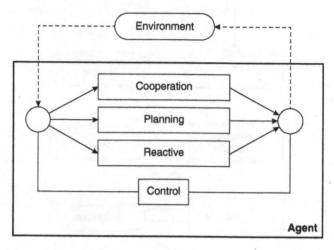

Figure 2.5   Vertical layered architecture.

action can then be decided by the top layer or the computation can be reversed back to the initial module. In this approach various layers can implement various levels of abstraction, e.g. behavioral, planning, social, etc. Figure 2.6 shows a horizontally layered agent model with three layers.

The advantages of layered approaches are their modularity. One can replace a single module layer without redesigning the entire agent. On the other hand they tend to be complex and require more effort in design, testing, and computational power at runtime.

An optional property of software agents, not mentioned so far, is mobility. Mobile agents, which have the ability of migrating between the computational environments while preserving its state and data, are a separate field of study. Technically, two types of migration are distinguished. We talk about *strong migration* when the agent resumes its computation from the very next instruction after migration call. *Weak migration* means resuming computation from the last checkpoint.

The incentive to move agents around are:

- resource optimization
- latency reduction by obtaining proximity to other agents and services
- optimizing network traffic by moving code rather than large volumes of data

Agent exchange information is based on asynchronous message passing and most agent communication languages have their roots in the *speech act theory*, developed by Austin [1975] and Searle and Searle [1969].

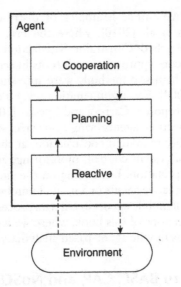

Figure 2.6   Horizontal layered architecture.

One important assumption of this theory is to consider language as an action rather then just the communication medium. According to Austin, the act of saying something (*locutionary act*) is a different category than the planned meaning of this act (*illocutionary act*) and then the planned effect of the act (*perlocutionary act*).

In the world of agents, where we don't have direct API calls, but rather a communication between autonomous entities, this approach is directly applicable. To achieve the desired outcome an agent has to consider how to formulate each particular message and how it will most likely be perceived by the recipient. Advanced schemas exist based on planning algorithms where acts of speech are the possible actions out of which an agent builds a plan to convince other agents about some facts or to persuade them to take up some actions. Cohen and Perrault [1979].

Popular MAS protocols, such as FIPA ACL, also use this theory, which is reflected for example in the use of so called *performatives*, i.e. verbs indicating the intention of the message, which have been identified in the research on speech act theory and which help software agents to understand the message semantics and follow the threads of conversations.

Building further on this communication foundation, agents use more sophisticated protocols to facilitate collaborative problem solving. Among the most important, one can identify task assignment, distributed planning, negotiation, or argumentation. Examples of distributed planning can be STRIPS-MA, Nissim et al. [2010], where the task is translated into the well known and researched Constraint Satisfaction Problem (CSP). For negotiations, game theory approaches with roots in economy were classically used, while ML and heuristic methods were introduced by the AI line of research. Lai et al. [2004]. For argumentation several dedicated theories and protocols have been proposed. Carrera and Iglesias [2015].

To conclude this section, agents bring a powerful set of paradigms, which brings a lot of flexibility to system construction, at the same time imposing challenges in terms of system control, monitoring, algorithm convergence and system state interpretation. Depending on the agent model we can create swarms of simple reactive agents or a limited number of highly specialized entities. Applications of mobile agents in big data processing and analytics will be shown in several sections of this book, where we will look at analogies to cloud systems as well as mobile agent-based analytics systems.

2.3   From ACID to BASE, CAP, and NoSQL – The Database (R)evolution

Another shift of paradigms in the last decades has taken place in the area of database systems. This movement is tightly connected to the shift of computing architectures towards distributed and asynchronous computations. As more and more data is processed independently by separate entities the traditional database transaction properties of ACID (Atomicity, Consistency, Independence, Durability) are no longer applicable.

An alternative to ACID is the BASE (Basically Available, Soft state, Eventually consistent) model. It puts emphasis on availability, while allowing for approximate answers and weakening of consistency.

Furthermore, in highly distributed systems the CAP theorem holds, Brewer [2000], which states that at a given time only two out of the following three properties can be achieved:

- consistency (all nodes see the same data at the same time)
- availability (a guarantee that every request receives a response about whether it was successful or if it has failed)
- partition tolerance (the system continues to operate despite arbitrary message loss or failure of part of the system)

Depending on the particular application we have to choose, which properties are more important for us? For example in a DNS system, which needs to be highly available and partition tolerant, we have to give up consistency, so that the information about a new physical address will take time to be distributed. On the other hand, in financial systems such as the ATM network or bank transfers, we will need to keep consistency but at the price of either distribution or high availability. Indeed, as a bank client we can tolerate an unavailable ATM, as long as there are many of them and our account balance is right.

Another aspect of the database layer which is changing, is that as the service granularity grows, the heterogeneity of database models also increases. Services with their defined APIs impose a natural boundary, which allows the internal information to be stored in a format independent of the outside world. The paradigm shift we described above was in line with the advent of NoSQL databases—a movement which introduced a variety of databases departing from relational models and specialized and optimized for specific tasks.

There is no one classification of NoSQL database family but typically we recognize the following types. DB-engines [2019]:

- Key-Value Stores (e.g. Redis, Memcached, Amazon DynamoDB, Riak KV, Ehcache)
- Wide Column Stores (e.g. Cassandra, HBase, Accumulo)
- Document Stores (e.g. MongoDB, Couchbase, CouchDB, Amazon DynamoDB, MarkLogic)
- Graph DBMS (e.g. Neo4j, OrientDB, Titan, Virtuoso, ArangoDB)
- RDF Stores (e.g. MarkLogic, Virtuoso, Jena, Sesame, AllegroGraph)
- Native XML DBMS (e.g. MarkLogic, Virtuoso, Sedna)
- Content Stores (e.g. Jackrabbit, ModeShape)
- Search Engines (e.g. Elasticsearch, Solr, Splunk, MarkLogic, Sphinx)

Key-value stores are based on a simple concept of storing key-value pairs and allowing for fast retrieval of values for a given key. This model is too simple to support a complex system on its own. However, for specific applications (e.g. managing the session information in web applications) it outperforms other more sophisticated solutions.

A somewhat more complex concept is introduced by Wide Column Stores. They give up a fixed schema by allowing storage of a very large number of dynamically added columns. As opposed to relational databases, data is not grouped by rows but by column families. This allows for fast aggregate/sort operations of such families. Other advantages include height scalability or the ability to update individual columns. Column stores give very fast access similar to key-value stores, but allow for more complex structure of data and, therefore, are used in more sophisticated scenarios, e.g. recommender systems or real time bidding for advertising.

Document stores introduce a schema-free approach. They can be considered as a subclass of key-values stores. The number and type of columns for each row can differ. It is also possible to store multi-value and nested structures. This allows storage of formats such as JSON without the need for parsing the structure on read/writes.

If we want to store graph data, which can be mapped to a node/edge structure, we can use dedicated Graph DBMS. Such engines not only allow storage of data in graph format, but also provide graph-specific operations such as path calculation etc. Graph databases are often based on a key-value store with the addition of the relationship concept.

The Semantic Web movement has introduced the Resource Description Framework (RDF) format and methodology for describing information. The structure of RDF data is to some extent similar to a graph structure. In order to manage this information RDF stores were created, which typically support also querying with SPARQL and sometimes provide means for descriptive logic reasoning.

As XML has become one of the most popular formats for data, database engines specifically designed for this purpose have also been introduced. While it is possible to store XML in other engines, e.g. relational, it is convenient to preserve their hierarchical structure and support XML specific query languages, e.g. XQuery.

Other widely used data formats data are related to digital multimedia contents. Content stores provide dedicated storage for such data. It is not sufficient to store just a picture or movie, but there is usually also some valuable metadata related to it. Content stores allow for maintenance of such meta information and indexing and querying of it.

Finally, we can distinguish search engines as a separate family of database systems. Their purpose is to optimize the search for information which best matches a given user query. Simple indexing provided by other DBMS engines is not sufficient, since we want to find entries which can match partially with the query (full text search) or even if the words are used in their different forms (stemming).

While this rich catalog of modern databases empowers engineers to build efficient and scalable solutions, one has to be aware of the limitations of these technologies. Various approaches, not only to database schema, but also other aspects such as transactions and consistency, means creators of computer systems will need other means for ensuring system reliability.

2.4   The Cloud

Cloud computing is yet another trend which has emerged in the last decades and has transformed the way enterprises store and process their data. Taking advantage of low hardware costs and high speed connections, vendors could deliver hosted services over the Internet, based on the pay-as-you-go approach. Mahmood and Hill [2011]. This appeals to both enterprises, which can shorten their time-to-market by skipping lengthy hardware provisioning and deployment, as well as startups, who can verify their business model before making significant investments. In general, companies can benefit from concentrating on their core business, while reducing the staff dedicated to infrastructure maintenance. On-demand scalability of cloud computing allows adaptation to the changing business needs, customer demands and new opportunities.

A cloud computing environment provides computing resources in a self-service, on-demand fashion. Furthermore, capabilities for dynamic, automatic scaling of resources based on the actual demand are possible. There are also monitoring tools providing metrics regarding performance of the computation jobs.

The main models for cloud computing can be divided into: Infrastructure as a Service (IaaS) – hardware including storage, virtual servers etc; Platform as a Service (PaaS) – environment for development and deployment of services; and Software as a Service (SaaS) – providing a service performing specific functionality (e.g. email, ERP, etc.). This family has been extending further and includes also Database as a Service (DBaas), Testing as a Service (TaaS), and several other models.

We can distinguish public, private, and hybrid clouds. Public clouds are run by cloud providers (e.g. Amazon Web Services, Microsoft Azure), who make the resources available to their customers. The pricing is usually based on the actual usage of the resources. Private clouds are clouds located within the enterprises that run them. Such a model gives more control over the infrastructure allowing for optimizing for specific needs. Data privacy issues are also less of a concern in this situation. However, it requires more effort and maintenance of specialized staff and data centers (often more then one for fault tolerance).

Recently a hybrid approach is gaining wider popularity. Here, enterprises maintain both their own private cloud and allocate some resources in the public cloud. In the case of sudden demand in computational power, e.g. Black Friday in an e-commerce scenario, the public part of the cloud can scale up to support the temporary needs. When the demand lowers the computation is again performed mainly in the private part.

One of the advantages of using cloud computing is the reduction of costs of the IT infrastructure. A cloud service provider can significantly reduce the unit costs by pooling and optimizing the use of a large number of servers in data centers. Also operational costs can be reduced by IT task centralization and automation.

The main challenges concerning cloud computing include security and privacy of data stored in the cloud, SLA of services deployed in the cloud especially when delivered to users scattered across various geographical locations, management of the entire operations consisting of several components: the cloud, on premise, mobile, etc.

Because the increasing proportion of data is stored in the cloud, the means for analytics of this data also need to adapt to this setup. According to Talia [2013] data analytics in the cloud can be performed in three different models, namely SaaS, PaaS, or IaaS:

- data analytics software as a service – provides a well-defined data mining algorithm or ready-to-use knowledge discovery tool as an Internet service to end users, who can access it directly through a Web browser

- data analytics platform as a service – provides a supporting platform that developers can use to build their own data analytics applications or extend existing ones without concern about the underlying infrastructure or distributed computing issues

- data analytics infrastructure as a service – provides a well-defined data mining algorithm or ready-to-use knowledge discovery tool as an Internet service to end users, who can access it directly through a Web browser

To provide analytic capabilities, cloud platforms incorporate additional tools like MapReduce algorithms or Machine Learning frameworks to be run directly in the cloud on the data uploaded there. Especially MapReduce became a framework which gained significant popularity among cloud service providers. Hashem et al. [2015]. A large effort has been made in order to provide SQL interfaces with the underlying MapReduce in order to facilitate easy, scalable access to the data stored in the cloud. We will elaborate more on this model in Chapter 7 devoted to big data analytics.

While cloud computing facilitates storage of the very large data sets, it imposes new challenges on processing and analytics of this data. This is the case especially where a public cloud is concerned. It is relatively easy to move large off-line computations, e.g. MapReduce jobs into the cloud. However, when real-time or interactive analytics needs to be performed, the speed of accessing the data becomes critical.

In order to provide high availability of the data stored in the cloud to the users located across various geographical locations, cloud providers need to work hard on optimizing the location of their data centers and potentially move the data between them as the demand changes. In the case of really dense data streams, e.g. clickstream, which we would like to analyze in real time, e.g. for fraud detection, uploading the data into the cloud and returning useful analytics in near real time is often impossible with the current technologies.

After describing cloud paradigms and models, we will conclude cloud related topics for now. More detailed description on cloud-based big data architectures will be presented in Chapter 5 dedicated entirely to this topic.

2.5 From Distributed Sensor Networks to the Internet of Things and Cyber-Physical Systems

So far in this book we have concentrated on the software side of the information systems. Yet, as we live in a physical world, all the business systems are in one way or another related to the events taking place around us. Humans have invented several devices that detect and measure such events, but for a long time there existed a gap between the ability to measure and perform computations based on this data. Sensors were expensive, scarce, and had limited computational power themselves and the network connectivity was slow.

The first systems concentrating on computations over sensor data were Distributed Sensor Networks (DSN) and later Wireless Sensor Networks (WSN). At the beginning their applications were limited to complex industry or military installations but became more widespread as the technology matured and the prices dropped. The big conceptual shift brought by WSN was that instead of carefully positioning complex sensors as close as possible to the observed phenomena, it enabled deployment of a large number of simpler nodes over the area of interest and analyzed the data gathered through ad-hoc networks formed between the nodes. This approach is much more suitable for dynamic environments such as battlefields, animal habitats, etc.

As the hardware cost dropped, computational power rose and the network connectivity improved, the number of devices equipped with sensors and actuators increased. Physical devices started gaining their own intelligence and were connected directly to the Internet resources. Soon this phenomenon started to go by the the the name of the Internet of Things (IoT), which was initially coined within the RFID community to describe the ability to track the location of physical objects.

As various software and hardware components became more tightly connected, another concept of Cyber-Physical Systems (CPS) has also emerged. According to one of the most compact definitions, *Cyber-Physical Systems are integrations of computations with physical processes.* Lee [2006]. Lee et al. [2015] propose a unified 5-level architecture as a guideline for implementation of a CPS. The goal of the architecture is to define, through a sequential work-flow manner, how to construct a CPS from the initial data acquisition, to the analytics, to the final value creation. From the bottom up, the following layers are distinguished:

- Smart connection level – manages the data acquisition process, by choosing the relevant sensors and providing seamless data integration.
- Data-to-information conversion level – provides semantics and analytics to the available data. Machine level applications such as health management can be implemented at this level.
- Cyber level – central level at which machines interact with each other forming the CPS.
- Cognition level – enables decision-making, simulation, and diagnostics on the CPS level.
- Configuration level – provides supervisory control and feedback about the entire system.

The two concepts, IoT and CPS, overlap and there is no clean division between them. However, looking at various definitions, one can risk a distinction that IoT is more focused on connectivity, time series analytics and realization of collaborative behaviors. CPS on the other hand, is concerned more with the high level relationship between the physical objects and computational algorithms. Thus, some claim IoT is an enabler for a broader goal of CPS. Carruthers [2014].

It is also worth acknowledging the relationship between IoT and CPS and other domains or research areas such as Mobile Computing (MC), Pervasive Computing (PC), or Wireless Sensor Networks (WSN). While they emerged from different needs and different communities, they are also centered around maintaining control over and performing computation within physically distributed systems. Later in the book we will focus mostly around IoT as the most capacious term, which covers to some extent the other ones. Specifically, we will come back to those topics, when talking about sources of data (Chapter 3) and physically distributed big data systems (Chapter 8).

2.6 The Rise of Big Data

In the previous sections of this chapter we have seen how IT paradigms and environments evolved over the last decades, challenged by the growing requirements for data processing, up to the point where things changed so dramatically, we needed to give this phenomenon a name. This gave rise to the term of big data, which became one of the hottest topics referred to in computer science, economy, artificial intelligence, and a multitude of other disciplines, which benefited from it. Several of those applications in science and industry can be found in Chapter 4 on big data tasks.

The most common definition of the term big data refers to the situations when the amount of data becomes overwhelming and cannot be handled by traditional database and computation technologies. One of the most common definitions of big data refers to the so called 4 Vs namely: Volume, Variety, Velocity, and Veracity. IBM.

The first V, Volume, naturally comes from the name and describes the key challenge. The volumes of data counted in PB are no longer shocking nowadays. As the data comes from many different sources, in many different formats, structured, semi-structured and unstructured, the problem of variety arises. It is not feasible to fuse the data as it comes, but a tedious task of structuring and integration is needed. Velocity of the data is yet another problem. Events generated in microservices, sensors, web page impressions, market transactions, etc. flow in very dense streams, sometimes requiring response within milliseconds. Finally, Veracity represents the fact that data is not perfect. It can come incomplete, with errors or with directly contradicting facts.

There are also 6 Vs, 10 Vs, and other models, but rather then split hairs and discuss how many properties we should account for, we will move on with more practical topics. In the reminder of the book we will look at how to tackle these challenges by building scalable big data architectures, able to handle high volumes of data coming at a fast pace from various sources in various formats and unknown quality.

CHAPTER 3
Sources of Data

A
s mentioned in Chapter 1, the big variety of data coming from diverse sources is one of the key properties of the big data phenomenon. It is, therefore, beneficial to understand how data is generated in various environments and scenarios, before looking at what should be done with this data and how to design the best possible architecture to accomplish this.

The evolution of IT architectures, described in Chapter 2, means that the data is no longer processed by a few big monolith systems, but rather by a group of services. In parallel to the processing layer, the underlying data storage has also changed and became more distributed. This in turn required a significant paradigm shift as the traditional approach to transactions (ACID) could no longer be supported. On top of this, cloud computing is becoming a major approach with the benefits of reducing costs and providing on-demand scalability but at the same time introducing concerns about privacy, data ownership, etc.

In the meantime the Internet continues its exponential growth. Every day both structured and unstructured data is published and available for processing. To achieve competitive advantage companies have to relate their corporate resources to external services, e.g. financial markets, weather forecasts, social media, etc. While several of the sites provide some sort of API to access the data in a more orderly fashion, countless sources require advanced web mining and Natural Language Processing (NLP) processing techniques.

Advances in science push researchers to construct new instruments for observing the universe or conducting experiments to understand even better the laws of physics and other domains. Every year humans have at their disposal new telescopes, space probes, particle accelerators, etc. These instruments generate huge streams of data, which need to be stored and analyzed.

The constant drive for efficiency in the industry motivates the introduction of new automation techniques and process optimization. This could not be done without analyzing the precise data that describe these processes. As more and more human tasks are automated, machines provide rich data sets, which can be analyzed in real time to drive efficiency to new levels.

Finally, it is now evident that the growth of the Internet of Things is becoming a major source of data. More and more of the devices are equipped with significant computational power and can generate a continuous data stream from their sensors.

In the subsequent sections of this chapter we will look at the domains described above to see what they generate in terms of data sets. We will compare the volumes but will also look at what is characteristic and important from their respective points of view.

3.1   The Internet

The Internet is undoubtedly the largest database ever created by humans. While several well described, cleaned, and structured data sets have been made available through this medium, most of the resources are of an ambiguous, unstructured, incomplete or even erroneous nature. Still, several examples in the areas such as opinion mining, social media analysis, e-governance, etc., clearly show the potential lying in these resources. Those who can successfully mine and interpret the Internet data can gain unique insight and competitive advantage in their business.

An important area of data analytics on the edge of corporate IT and the Internet is Web Analytics. The field is devoted to collecting the data regarding web traffic on the web sites and using it to gain insight about patterns on user navigation, UI efficiency, etc. In research publications, such analysis also goes by the name of Web Usage Mining, Srivastava et al. [2000], as the task of analyzing logs from Internet servers to find patterns in how the users navigate through the World Wide Web (WWW). While the fundamental information can be collected from locally maintained analytical software, the nature of surfing the Web requires going beyond the on-premise resources.

In today's Internet, search engines are the main power distributing the traffic in various directions. Therefore, information about what people search for is of the highest importance. In many companies, especially in areas such as e-commerce, activities devoted to Search Engine Optimization (SEO) and Search Engines Marketing (SEM) are mission critical.

3.1.1   The Semantic Web

As mentioned above, vast amounts of interesting and rich data sources are located in the Web. Since most of it is unstructured and hard to process automatically, there have been many efforts to impose some form of structure and semantics. By far the most significant of these efforts is the Semantic Web. It is the extension of the WWW that enables people to share content beyond the boundaries of applications and websites. The Semantic Web enables data to be linked from a given source to any other source and to be understood by computers.

The Semantic Web is built upon three main standards, Hendler [2009]:

- RDF (Resource Description Framework): the data modeling language for the Semantic Web. All Semantic Web information is stored and represented in the RDF.
- SPARQL (SPARQL Protocol and RDF Query Language): the query language of the Semantic Web. It is specifically designed to query data across various systems.
- OWL (Web Ontology Language) The schema language, or knowledge representation (KR) language, of the Semantic Web

The model Semantics Web Stack is shown in Figure 3.1 and consists of several layers. The foundations are based on well known Hypertext Web technologies, i.e. URI, Unicode, XML. The middle layers contain W3C standards

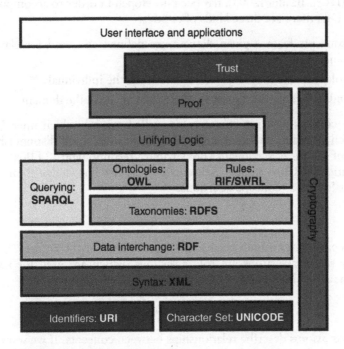

Figure 3.1 Semantic web stack.
Source: https://commons.wikimedia.org/wiki/File:Semantic_web_stack.svg. Public domain

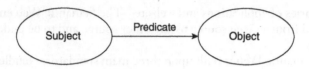

Figure 3.2   RDF graph.

out of which RDF, PARQL, and OWL mentioned above are the most important. Finally, the top layers give the value to the semantic data users by providing reasoning and trust capabilities. These top functionalities are still lacking final standardization and convincing solutions.

RDF provides a graph-based framework for structuring data as statements about resources. Each RDF statement is a triple consisting of: Subject (resource), Predicate (property), and Object (value). Figure 3.2 shows the graph representation of a RDF triple.

A powerful feature of using structured semantic knowledge is the possibility for automated reasoning with such data. A special group of Description Logics (DLs), Baader [2003], has been developed in order to accomplish this task. In DLs there are three kinds of entities:

- concepts from a given domain are defined and used for classifying objects and describing their properties
- roles represent binary relations between the individuals
- individual names represent single individuals in the domain

DL consists of a set of statements called axioms, which must be true in a given situation. While it is not obligatory, usually, we distinguish three groups of axioms: assertional (ABox) axioms, terminological (TBox) axioms, and relational (RBox) axioms. ABox axioms capture knowledge about named individuals such as concept assertions:

$$Student(john)$$

which means that an individual john is an instance of the concept Student. Another set of assertions are role assertions, which are used for relations between named individuals. For example:

$$supervisorOf(paul, john)$$

TBox axioms describe relationships between concepts. If we want to say all students are persons we will write:

$$Student \sqsubseteq Person$$

We use RBox axioms for properties of roles. For example we can state that

$$supervisorOf \sqsubseteq coworker$$

In DLs more complex concepts can be build from axioms with the use of constructors. The basic constructors are conjunction $(A \sqcup B)$, disjunction $(A \sqcap B)$, and complement $(\neg A)$. DLs can be further extended to include commonsense reasoning, e.g. by embedding default logics. While out of the scope of this book, its worth mentioning that attempts have been made to set up a distributed reasoning framework for description logic with the use of multi-agent paradigms. Wiech et al. [2011].

Despite well defined standards and efforts made by some big public and private organizations, the adoption of the Semantic Web is still limited. Countless valuable resources remain unstructured or semi-structured. One of the reasons is the large effort needed to maintain the data in a structured form. Also the amount of experts fluent in the Semantic Web technologies is still limited. Finally, not everybody sees the full potential of automated processing and reasoning with semantic knowledge.

3.1.2 Linked Data

Linked data is a newer and more practical concept than the Semantic Web. Basically it is a set of best practices for easy sharing of data in the Web. Standards and technologies of the Semantic Web, e.g. OWL, RDF, SPARQL can be used to build linked data solutions. Berners-Lee proposed the following set of rules, which are now commonly known as the "linked data principles." Berners-Lee [2006]:

1. Use URIs as names for things
2. Use HTTP URIs so that people can look up those names
3. When someone looks up a URI, provide useful information, using the standards (RDF, SPARQL)
4. Include links to other URIs, so that they can discover more things

RDF links between things are realized as triples, e.g.:

```
Subject:http://data.linkedmdb.org/resource/film/77
Predicate:http://www.w3.org/2002/07/owl#sameAs
Object:http://dbpedia.org/resource/Pulp_Fiction_film
```

To date the largest effort to adopt the linked data principles has been the Linking Open Data project W3C. Its goal is to identify open data resources, convert them to RDF, and publish for wide use on the Web.

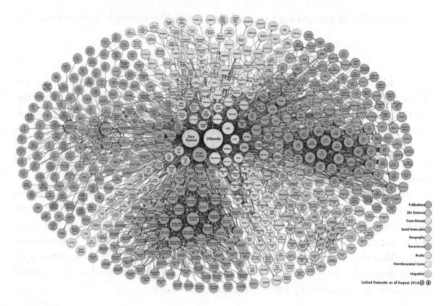

Figure 3.3   LOD cloud.
Source: Max Schmachtenberg, Christian Bizer, Anja Jentzsch, and Richard Cyganiak.
August 2014. https://commons.wikimedia.org/wiki/File:LOD_Cloud_2014-08.svg.
Licensed under CC-BY SA 3.0.

The LOD cloud diagram depicted in Figure 3.3 has become the icon of the project and of the linked data and the Semantic Web in general.

On top of published linked data resources an ecosystem of applications has been created. This includes:

- Linked data browsers – give the possibility to navigate across data following RDF based links
- Linked data search engines – index the linked data content and allow search by keyword of relevant resources, which can be further browsed with the use of linked data browsers
- Domain specific tools – very often mash-ups of linked data sources, e.g. DBPedia Mobile. Becker and Bizer [2008].

3.1.3   Knowledge Graphs

The big effort towards structuring of knowledge from various sources has been made by Google by introducing the Knowledge Graph. Singhal [2012]. With the use of structured knowledge sources like Freebase, Bollacker et al. [2008], Wikipedia, or CIA World Factbook, as well as data indexed by Google, the Knowledge Graph allows searching for specific entities, e.g. people, countries, movies, etc. Formally we can define a knowledge graph in the following way:

Definition 1:   A knowledge graph $G = (V; E)$ is a labeled graph with nodes representing entities and edges representing various relations between entities. The labeling function will be denoted as l. Each entity is associated with a set of types/classes, and the classes form a class hierarchy via the *subClass* relation.

On such defined graphs we can run queries

Definition 2:   A graph query is a labeled graph $Q = (V_Q; E_Q)$.

To process such queries a structured query language can be used such as SPARQL, introduced in Chapter 2, and graph pattern matching through to techniques like keyword searches. While the use of a structured language allows more precise conditions to be specified, it also requires knowledge of the data schema. On the other hand a keyword search gives more freedom but introduces more ambiguity and takes less advantage of the data structure. Graph pattern matching techniques fall in between these extremes and can provide a good balance between structured and unstructured approaches. Su et al. [2015].
A binary relation $R \subseteq V_q \times V$ is a *match* if

1. for each $(u, v) \in R$, u and v have the same label, i.e., $l_Q(u) = l_G(v)$
2. for each edge $(u, u') \in E_q$, there exists an edge $(v, v') \in E$ such that $(u', v') \in R$

Automated creation of large knowledge graphs is a very difficult task. While it is relatively easy to extract a sizable collection of interrelated facts, making it useful knowledge is not straightforward. Pujara et al. [2013] describe the process of knowledge graph identification, which is defined as removing noise, inferring missing information, and determining which candidate facts should be included into the knowledge graph. The authors propose application of Probabilistic Soft Logic (PSL) as a tool for efficient knowledge graph identification.

Knowledge graphs can be used by machine learning algorithms to extract useful knowledge. A review of Statistical Relational Learning (SRL) methods can be found in Nickel et al. [2015].

3.1.4 Social Media

There are several data sources in the Internet, which are inherently of unstructured nature. A good example is social media. Even though there is an overlying pattern, like the network of friends on Facebook or chain of tweets and re-tweets on Twitter, the data itself is of highly unstructured nature. Convenient API provided by many social media platforms does not help much with this problem. However, if we can process and give semantics to this data its value for many applications is huge.

Usage of the most popular social media platforms in July 2019 can be found in Table 3.1 (for up to date statistics check statista.com).

Interestingly, the majority of the data for social media big data comes from Twitter. One of the main reasons for such a state of affairs is the availability of data on this platform. Other social media channels, e.g. Facebook, limit visibility of the majority of the content to the general audience. Moreover, Twitter data is relatively easy to process. The size limit of a single tweet is 280 characters (doubled from 140 in 2017) which, by default, makes the messages concise. Twitter users use also *hashtags*, which provide explicit tagging, grouping and therefore additional semantics to the text. Finally, there is good API and a large set of tools and libraries ready to be used to kick off a Twitter analysis.

3.1.5 Web Mining

Several efforts have been made in order to automate the process of extracting from the Web the data which lacks metadata or any semantic layer provided

Table 3.1 Social media users.

Site	Users (mln)	Site	Users (mln)
Facebook	2375	Sina Weibo	465
YouTube	2000	Reddit	330
WhatsApp	1600	Twitter	330
Facebook Messenger	1300	Douban	320
WeChat	1112	Linkedin	310
Instagram	1000	Snapchat	294
QQ	823	Pinterest	265
QZone	572	Viber	260
Douyin/Tik Tok	500	Discord	250

by the publisher. Quite often it is possible to reverse engineer the structure by discovering patterns in the HTML tag hierarchy.

An interesting example of a service implementing this idea is import.io. This startup provides tools to add meaning to particular elements of web pages and then by taking advantage of repeating patterns automates the extraction of data, even if they are paginated or nested in lined subpages. Furthermore, a JSON API can be automatically created which can be plugged into a production service architecture and feed the data in real time.

The most popular approach nowadays is the use of general purpose search engines. Sites like Google.com, Yahoo.com, and Ask.com provide tools for ad-hoc queries based on keywords and page rankings. Some of them put an API layer on top of their engine, so one can integrate them with corporate systems, although this may require paid access. The advantage of these tools, being general purpose, is at the same time their drawback. This approach, while very helpful on a day-to-day basis, is not sufficient to search for large amounts of specialized information.

In Kogut et al. [2013] a multi-agent system for retrieval of scientific information from heterogeneous sources is presented. It shows how the use of general purpose search engines and direct access to specialized databases such as DBLP can be applied to search for scientific information in the Internet. In order to set up such a data sourcing system with the seamless integration of the data, several issues have to be resolved:

- multiple data access methods - JSON APIs, XML APIs, HTML, etc.
- mapping of the data elements between the sources
- merging the data
- tracking changes in all of the above and the data itself

Another approach to the problem of retrieving valuable data from the Internet is to create crawlers, which search for pages related to a predefined subject. If we perform the process by ourselves, we can have an influence on the document selection or the depth of the search. A special case of web harvesting is focused crawling. This method, introduced by Chakrabarti et al. [1999], uses some labeled examples of relevant documents, which serve as a starting point in the search for new resources.

Other possibilities for accessing web content is subscribing to RSS (Really Simple Syndication) feeds. RSS is a XML-based format for sharing and distributing updates to web pages. There is a large number of aggregators, which allows users to subscribe to feeds of their choice and produce a compilation of relevant updates and news.

3.2 Scientific Data

3.2.1 Biomedical Data

Biomedical data is one of the fastest growing sources of information in the world. In particular the domain of health provides a plethora of data sources as well as numerous scenarios for their applications. Advances in genome sequencing, growing number of wearables, medical microsensors, real-time imaging, and many others add to the already huge data assets. And it does not stop here as, from the public health perspective, collecting relevant environmental information is also important. Andreu-Perez et al. [2015].

Electronic Health Records (EHR) are one of the best sources of medical data. It is estimated that out of millions of patients under some medical system, each of them generates on average about 1000 health events over 3 years. Hemingway et al. [2017]. Such cross-population databases are extremely valuable, as they allow the study of some rare medical conditions, which occur only once in hundreds of thousands of patients.

Some of the richest medical insights can be derived by real time imaging. Nowadays, a human body can be scanned with frequencies ranging from MHz (MRI), through optical rage and X-ray to EHz (PET). Ever increasing resolutions result in sizes of individual scans reaching terabytes. For example a whole body CT scan can take 750 MB, while a microscopic human brain scan 66 TB. Scholl et al. [2011].

Human DNA is comprised of approximately 3 billion base pairs, which results in approximately 100 GB of data about the personal genome. With the cost of genome sequencing dropping below $1000 per genome, databases devoted to studying genetic variations are growing rapidly. Buchanan et al. [2012]. The dropping cost of a single genome sequencing procedure is shown in Figure 3.4.

In Stephens et al. [2015] the authors compare genomics to astronomy, YouTube, and Twitter, and claim that in terms of acquisition, storage, distribution, and analysis, genomics will provide the same or even more challenges than the other sources with am estimated 1 ZB (Zetta Bytes)/year generated by 2025.

The first breakthrough was made with the sequencing of the first human genome under the *Human Genome Project (HGP)*. Since the turn of the century several further initiatives have been launched to utilize the new opportunities. *1000 Genomes Project* started in 2008 to sequence the entire genomes of 1000 people. Kuehn [2008]. *ENCODE* was designed to map and characterize how the entire human genome functions. Consortium et al. [2012].

In recent years the increasing availability of such biomedical data has opened up new possibilities for personalized medicine programs. Costa [2014].

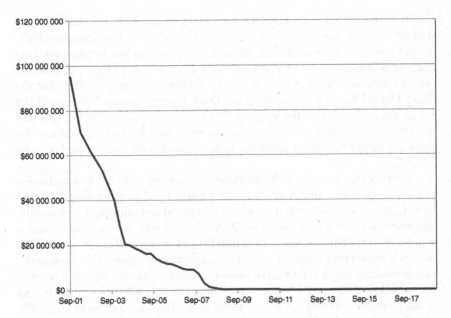

Figure 3.4   The cost of sequencing per genome over time.

Scientists can perform analyses on entire populations to find patterns and help design drugs. Their results can then be matched with an individual genome to choose an approach suited for the particular patient.

Apart from medicine, other fields of research such as agriculture also benefit greatly from the genomic data, as improved health of crops and livestock directly increases the profitability.

Medical sensors are also becoming an important source of data. As they belong to a larger family of devices, we will discuss them under the Internet of Things in Section 3.4.

3.2.2   Physics and Astrophysics Data

Astronomy has a long tradition of dealing with large data sets and finding smart ways for distributing it. A good example is the SETI@home program launched in 1999, which uses Internet-connected computers to analyze radio telescope data in order to find narrow-bandwidths. Such unnatural radio impulses could come from extraterrestrial intelligence. The statistics of the project are impressive, with over 5 million users and over 2 million years of aggregated computing. The project has paved the way for many other collaborative computing initiatives running on a common BOINC (Berkeley Open Infrastructure for Network Computing) platform Berkeley.

In recent years the nature of astronomical research has shifted from studying specific targets to large sky surveys and then conducting multiple studies over the collected data. Several of these studies require tracking changes in observations, so the scans are repeated over and over in order to produce time series. Zhang et al. [2015]. Examples of such projects are the Sloan Digital Sky Survey (SDSS), the Dark Energy Survey (DES), and the Large Synoptic Survey Telescope (LSST). The approach of systematic sky surveys produces extremely large data sets. For example, the LSST uses a telescope capturing 3.2 billion pixels per image. This results in daily load of some 140 TB.

Another type of large scale computations possible with big data technologies are large-scale simulations, e.g. the formation of galaxies. Feigelson and Babu [2012]. These simulations are later compared and calibrated with real life observations to verify the assumptions and hypotheses. An example of such a simulation is the Millennium Simulation Project performed at the Max Planck Society's Supercomputing Centre. The simulation involved 10 billion particles mimicking the distribution of matter in space. The experiment generated some 25 TB of data, which allowed scientists to gain a better understanding of the evolution of the galaxies and black holes. Boylan-Kolchin et al. [2009]. Visual results of the Millennium Simulation, Springel et al. [2005], can be admired in Figure 3.5.

The future will bring even more astronomical data, as old instruments are regularly replaced by new ones, which bring better image resolution. For example the James Webb Space Telescope will have 6.5 meter mirror compared to the Hubble Space Telescope's 2.4 meter mirror. Numerous other instruments will also be sent to space as well as constructed on earth, adding to the already rich stream of scientific information.

Another area of research producing very large amounts of data is High Energy Physics (HEP). HEP is a "participative" science, where various particles are disassembled in order to understand their internal structure. In contrast to astronomy (discussed earlier in the previous section) the data generated in this process is more tied to specific experiment and hardware setup and therefore more short-lived. However, with more and more sophisticated accelerators and improved detectors constantly being built, very large volumes of data are produced on a daily basis. Gray et al. [2012].

In the Large Hadron Collider (LHC) 600 million particles per second collide. As a result, detectors generate 1 PB of data per second, an amount that cannot be processed with any currently available technology. Therefore, decisions need to be made in real time about which data represent scientific value. It is expected that even after filtering 99% of the data, 50 PB will still have to be stored and processed every year. CERN [2017].

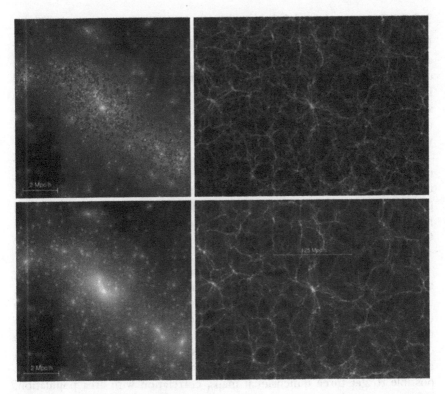

Figure 3.5   The millenium simulation.
Source: Springel et al. (2005). Reproduced with permission.

This case shows not only a large volume of data but also very challenging velocity, as during an experiment data flows from the sensors. In order to process all the data, the Worldwide LHC Computing Grid (WLCG) project has been initiated. It involves collaboration of more than 170 computing centers in 42 countries arranged in tiers. Tier-0, consisting of CERN Data Centre in Geneva and Wigner Research Centre for Physics in Budapest, works in direct connection with the LHC, while other tiers (1 to 2) allow more data and computation offloading. Tier 3 consists of local research clusters and individual scientist's machines.

With a new ambitious scientific agenda at CERN, which involves the next generation of High Luminosity LHC, the requirements for WLCG capacity will grow significantly in the coming years. It is forecast that data load will increase tenfold to 500 PB/year, outpacing the growth given by technological advances and, therefore, requiring new approaches and architectures to real time filtering and processing of data CERN.

3.2.3   Environmental Sciences

For a long time environmental sciences have relied on processing large amounts of information in order to provide tools and insights for geography, climate, agriculture, ecology, etc. Due to its nature, the domain has developed its own models and tools, which could capture the relevant aspects of the data such as geo-location, the physics of ocean currents and air masses, migration of animals, etc. All of these phenomena bring rich data sets, which grow each year with new measurement techniques and geo-distributed sensors.

Geographic data hwere gathered for centuries before the advent of computers, in order to facilitate the creation of maps, navigation, etc. However, the ability to store and analyze the data and the emergence of dedicated Geographical Information Systems (GIS), provided the real difference and opened new possibilities. Further on, people started to correlate data streams from GIS, satellites, ground sensors, and even social media, to fuse them into large scale big data systems.

An example of such a big data application is natural disaster warning and aid systems. With events such as tsunamis, hurricanes, earthquakes, etc. taking thousands of lives, it is crucial to send information and help to the impacted areas as soon as possible. Several data sources are available to tackle this task. Satellite images nowadays provide high resolution images of developing dangers, e.g. hurricanes as well as the impacts, landslides in difficult to access regions. By combining this data with GIS systems it is possible to get three dimensional maps, correlation with area population, information on local facilities such as electricity, water, etc. All of this can greatly speed up rescue missions, evacuation plans, supply logistics, and many other tasks.

Satellite imagery is one of the richest data sources. The longest-running satellite imagery program for the Earth is called Landsat. Since 1972 eight satellites gathered millions of images in multiple bands with spatial resolutions ranging from 15 to 60 meters. As of today Landsat satellites add around 700 GB of data every day adding to the total of 3 PB gathered so far. This pace will accelerate with the launch of Landsat-9 scheduled for 2020. NASA [2018]. The amount of aerial imagery is also growing thanks to the spread of Unmanned Aerial Vehicles (UAVs), which can be equipped with various sensors and can be dispatched much quicker and at lower cost then satellites.

While we will discuss sensor information in more detail later in this chapter, it is important to note the large number of environmental specific measurement instruments in use today. Meteorology has been, for decades, developing a network of measurement stations throughout the world, which provide temperature, pressure, humidity, wind speed, and other readings on a regular basis. Modern weather radars can locate and track the motion of rain, snow, and hail with very high precision. Seismographic stations around the world, connected into the Global Seismographic Network (GSN), provide timely information on earthquakes. Historical data gathered at Incorporated Research Institutions for Seismology (IRIS) amounts to hundreds of TB IRIS.

3.3 Industrial Data

While it is widely believed that big data will play a key role in the industry of the future, the possibilities of using it to create new value in various branches of industry varies. The McKinsey Global Institute has created the *Big Data Value Potential Index* to try to measure these differences. Manyika [2011]. The index aggregates five criteria that contribute the final estimate:

- Amount of data per firm – calculated as the storage available per firm (normalized by taking into account firms above 1000 employees to avoid data skew)
- Variability in performance – the difference between the 10th and 90th percentile EBITDA (earnings before interest tax depreciation and amortization) for major companies in each sector
- Customer and supplier intensity – the number of front-line employees (sales, administration) per firm (firms above 1000 employees)
- Transaction intensity – the amount of processing power (PCs and mainframes) of an average firm in a sector (firms above 1000 employees)
- Turbulence – the number of new companies placed in the top 20 ranking divided by 20

Figure 3.6 shows the big data value potential index against the ease-of-capture index after McKinsey Global Institute. The leaders are the financial and information sectors. The public sector has great potential due to huge and valuable data sets, but are slow to adapt new technologies. Health care, manufacturing, and retailing face limitations from fragmentation, resulting in limited data sets, but major players in those fields can make significant progress. Brown et al. [2011].

3.3.1 Smart Factories

In today's factories, machines are mostly connected, creating a collaborative organism. This evolution increases overall system complexity and requires advanced automated planning, monitoring, diagnostics, and recovery capabilities. Such environments fall into the category of Cyber-Physical Systems

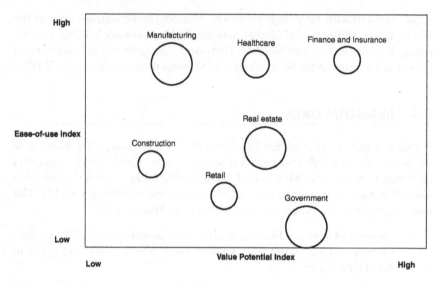

Figure 3.6   Big data value potential index.

(CPS) (as defined in Chapter 2) and the transformation is referred to as Industry 4.0.

Three types of integration can be distinguished in Industry 4.0. Firstly, *horizontal integration* refers to inter-company integration allowing for fluent flow of information, finance, and material. *Vertical integration*, on the other hand, describes integration between multiple actuator and sensor signals across different levels up to the Enterprise Resource Planning (ERP) system. Finally, *end-to-end engineering integration* represents the value creation path related to the product, ranging from customer requirements, all the way to maintenance and even recycling. Wang et al. [2016] .

All of the above integrations result in information flow between the systems. With more and more sensors deployed on the production floor this number is only going to grow. The total data footprint in industry scenarios can reach tens of TB yearly and more. Mourtzis et al. [2016].

Both big data and multi-agent systems have been considered as enabling technologies for Industry 4.0, with big data gaining wider adoption in recent years, but strongly inspired by the early ideas brought by MAS. Some of the major applications of agents in intelligent manufacturing systems include Shen et al. [2006]:

- Encapsulation of manufacturing activities or wrap legacy software systems

- Representation of physical manufacturing resources, aggregations of resources, products, parts, and operations
- Representation of negotiation partners
- Implementation of some special services in agent-based manufacturing system

3.3.2 SmartGrid

The energy market has been, in recent years, one of the most dynamically evolving industry sectors. Technological changes show their impact on each level of the power grid. Renewable energy sources affect not only generation but also transmission and distribution Efficient and safe operations of such a complex system requires next generation of controlling and monitoring systems. Simmhan et al. [2013].

The main source of data in the smart grid is the Advanced Metering Infrastructure (AMI). Table 3.2 shows the amount of data collected by 1 million metering devices in a year. Zhou et al. [2016].

Apart from smart meters, other devices are also sources of big data in utilities, e.g. distribution automation data (grid equipment), third-party data (off-grid data sets), and asset management data (firmware for all smart devices and associated operating systems), Outage Management Systems (OMS), Distribution Management Systems (DMS), Meter Data Management Systems (MDMS), etc. Witt [2014].

Renewable energy sources, such as wind or solar, are very dependent on weather conditions. Therefore, detailed weather data is yet another source of information needed for power generation forecasting, system fault identification, and user energy consumption forecasting, etc.

3.3.3 Aviation

The latest models of aircraft are built with more and more sensors, generating increasing volumes of data. A single jet engine can be equipped with thousands of sensors and generate tens of GB of data per second, while the entire aircraft can produce hundreds of TB during a single flight. Rapolu [2016]. It is

Table 3.2 The amount of data collected by 1 million metering devices in a year

Collection frequency	1/day	1/hour	1/30 min	1/15 min
Records (billion)	0.37	8.75	17.52	35.04
Volume of data (Tb)	1.82	730	1460	2920

estimated, that the global fleet could generate 98 million TB of data by 2026. Wyman [2016].

The main part of this data comes from Aircraft Health Monitoring systems (AHM) and Predictive Maintenance systems (PM) used for: Engine Condition Monitoring (ECM), airframe maintenance, component maintenance, etc. AHM systems can have both on-board based components, which gather the data from numerous sensors and provide their initial fusion and real time analytics, as well as on-the-ground part, which can aggregate more historical data and perform advanced analytical tasks.

The goal of predictive maintenance systems is to determine the best time for maintenance work to be performed. It should be done in order to ensure safety, while being cost efficient and avoiding unnecessary tasks, which can be costly. While the total number of airplanes or their engines is not very big, the number of parameters describing them can be huge, resulting in substantial data sets, especially if we combine them with other factors, such as environmental data, flight history, etc.

3.4   Internet of Things

The Internet of Things (IoT) has emerged as one of the fastest growing trends in IT in recent years. With the growing number of electronic circuits embedded in physical items and their increasing computational power and capabilities, the natural direction is to connect them and enable large scale interoperability and data exchange.

The definition of the IoT is very wide and ranges from RFID tags, beacons, wearable devices, through more complex sensors, vehicles, and entire buildings. Basically more and more physically distributed units are used to control objects and thus embed them into the software IT infrastructure. Based on such foundations, ideas such as intelligent homes, smart cities or smart grids can be accomplished.

In the IoT setup data can be exchanged in many different ways. One of the simplest ones is RFID, which enables electronic barcodes for identification of objects they are attached to. A special case of RFID is NFC (Near-Field Communication), which has adopted by some mobile phone manufacturers, and which provides a secure way for data to be exchanged. An NFC device is capable of being both an NFC reader and an NFC tag, which allows NFC devices to communicate peer-to-peer.

Data can also be obtained from Wireless Sensor Networks (WSN), which are composed of several efficient, low cost, low power, miniature devices for use in remote sensing applications. Nodes in WSN are able to collect data and then route it throughout the network to a specific data storage or processing node. Yet, through on-board microprocessors, sensor nodes can be programmed not only to transmit what they observe but also to accomplish more complex tasks. Akyildiz and Vuran [2010].

An important prerequisite for collecting data in the IoT is finding the devices available in the environment. This requires some way to address this: one the way is the use the Internet protocol in its latest version IPv6. The Constrained Application Protocol (Co AP) has made it possible to provide resource constrained devices with RESTful web service functionalities and consequently to integrate WSNs and smart objects with the Web. Colitti et al. [2011]. Other efforts are also being made in this area, e.g. EPICS Wikipedia, which is a standard for identifying objects in many industries.

The amount of data that the IoT produces means that storage, ownership, and expiry of the data become critical issues. Gubbi et al. [2013]. While big data and cloud solutions can provide infrastructure and tools for handling, processing, and analyzing the deluge of IoT data, we still need efficient methods and solutions that can structure, annotate, share, and make sense of the IoT data and facilitate transforming it to actionable knowledge and intelligence in different application domains. Barnaghi et al. [2012].

CHAPTER 4

Big Data Tasks

A fter defining the sources of big data in Chapter 2, we introduce the most important and challenging tasks and problems we want to solve. Using searching, through social media analysis, to smart grid control, today's real life systems require new approaches to handle big data. Those who neglect implementation of big data techniques will fail to solve the problems growing day by day or will have to give ground to the competition capable of disrupting the status quo.

In the following sections, we will go through some of the most challenging big data tasks in various branches of industry and science, which will prepare us to understand and dive into architectures capable of tackling those tasks later in Chapter 6. The selection of tasks is subjective and does not cover all branches of business and science, but I believe it gives a good overview of problems related to handling huge data sets in practice.

4.1 Recommender Systems

Recommender systems are one of the key e-commerce tools for increasing revenue by providing a personalized offer to its users. In 2006 Netflix was already willing to pay US$1 000 000 in a competition to predict user ratings for films. Bennett et al. [2007]. Since then several algorithms and systems have been developed and today one can choose among multiple solutions, libraries, and even *Recommendation as a Service* offerings.

At the time of the Netflix prize, the most important group of recommender methods were collaborative filtering algorithms. They were based on collecting the preferences of several users and assuming that if person A has the same opinion as person B on a certain issue, then A also is more likely to have B's opinion on a different issue. For example, if users A and B liked (and as a result bought) item X, then if user A also bought item Y, recommending Y to B would be a good option for a successful recommendation.

More formally we can model user ratings as a matrix

$$R^{|U| \times |I|}$$

where $U = u_1, u_2, \ldots, u_n$ is a set of users and $I = i_1, i_2, \ldots, i_m$ is a set of items, which we want to recommend.

At a given time we know only part (typically small) of all ratings. The tasks is then to find the best approximation

$$\hat{R}^{|U| \times |I|}$$

filling in the missing values.

For the world's largest marketplaces and other e-commerce sites the dimensions of the recommendations problem can be very big, with millions or even tens of millions of users and items. What is particularly difficult in practical applications, is that the matrix defined above is typically extremely sparse. In real world cases we may have to deal with more then 99% of missing values.

The problem becomes even more complex when we take into account the way user ratings were gathered. In general we distinguish between explicit and implicit feedback. In the first case, users "vote" by filling in an explicit rating field, therefore consciously providing their opinion. On the other hand in the implicit approach, we take into account various indirect "signals" coming from the interaction of the user with an item, e.g. viewing, putting into a basket, number of interactions, etc. It is not clear which type of feedback is better. The explicit feedback answers the question directly, but the answer might not be honest. On the other hand implicit feedback does not provide a direct answer, but is based on real actions and therefore should reflect more accurately real user intentions.

Another issue, which makes the recommendation system more complex, is the existence of *ephemeral items*. Examples of such cases are Internet auctions, where the same product can be described in different ways by different users, which creates explosion of the item dimension and creates even more sparse data sets.

For practical reasons, for certain users we can display only a limited number of recommended items. This defines the problem of finding top N items for a given user. Apart from collaborative filtering, mentioned previously, other methods include: content-based filtering, knowledge-based recommenders, and all types of hybrid systems.

4.2 Search

Traditionally *search engines* are regarded as the practical application of information retrieval techniques to large-scale text collections. Croft et al. [2010]. With exponentially growing repositories of all kinds of digital content, this no longer applies only to text but also to pictures, sound, videos, etc. The scope

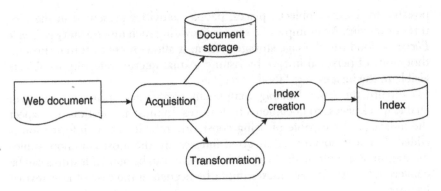

Figure 4.1   Search engine – indexing.

of a search can vary according to the application, e.g. Web search, enterprise search, etc. In order to facilitate efficient information retrieval, the search engine might have to perform other tasks on top of search, e.g. clustering of documents, filtering spam, tagging, etc.

The search task can be broken down into two major phases. Firstly an index is created. This process is depicted in Figure 4.1. The first building block, *document acquisition*, can be simple as in the case of readily available collections or very complex as in Web crawling or similar other scenarios. It is not feasible, from both time and storage perspectives, to index all Web documents. Therefore, some form of evaluation and pre-filtering has to be implemented here. Before putting them into storage, documents are annotated with relevant metadata.

The role of the *document transformation* component is extracting from the documents the relevant features. For text documents a natural level of indexing is a word, but we can add more power to the search engine by identifying phrases, dates, names, etc.

The *document transformation* phase can involve some additional steps of enriching the data. One of the possibilities is classification of documents based on their content. This can be done either by classification into some predefined classes, e.g. areas of interest, spam/non-spam, etc., or by clustering, which creates groups of similar documents but without a predefined label.

Other, non-textual types of documents have their own specific features. For example multimedia files can include valuable meta-data such as author, genre (movies), tags, etc. These can be processed as textual information, but with some readily available semantics. Also, some more *technical* features such as geo-location, resolution, etc. can be of value.

However, the most rich information can be available within the content of multimedia documents. By applying image recognition techniques, it is possible to discover objects, places, people, activities presented in the pictures or movies. An example of a service providing such functionality is *Google Photos*, a cloud based image storage system. It allows users to search through thousands of personal images by issuing textual queries referring to objects visible in the images, e.g. "food," "sea," etc.

Finally, the *Index Building* component creates data structures that will enable quick access to documents by features. In most applications we expect the indexes to be capable of being constantly rebuilt as new information is added. For text documents, inverted indexes are the most common implementation. For multimedia files, similar indexes can be build if features can be converted to text. Other indexes might be needed in the case of non-textual features.

The basis for building an index is gathering of relevant statistics. Those statistics relate to various counts, positions in document, as well as global statistics in the whole document corpus. Not all features are equally important, therefore specific weights are attributed to them. For text documents metrics such as *tf-idf (term frequency.inverse document frequency)* are used for the weighting purpose.

To ensure high efficiency of the system, indexes for groups of documents are distributed across multiple nodes. This allows scalable, distributed computations.

Once the index is in place, user queries can be handled effectively. As shown in Figure 4.2, the *user interaction* component is responsible for receiving the user query and transforming it into a request to the index. The *ranking* component returns the ranked list of results based on scores returned by a model. The *evaluation* is monitoring performance of the search tasks and allows tuning of the system.

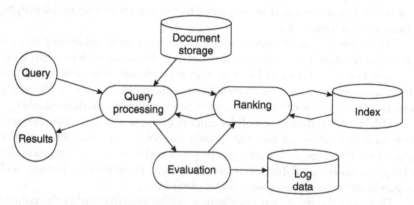

Figure 4.2 Search engine – query.

The first step taking place after a query is issued is its transformation. For text queries, which are most common, tokenizing, stopping, and stemming are the obvious initial tasks. For non-textual scenarios, other types of queries exist. For example it is possible to use a *query by example* strategy for multimedia, where the query is a media file. To process such a query it is necessary to extract features in the process similar to the document transformation described above and then use the relevant index to find the most similar files.

The main stage of the query process is performed by the ranking component. It takes the transformed query as an input and returns a ranked list of documents. Choosing the effective retrieval model is a complex task. In the most general form the document score can take the following form

$$\sum_i q_i d_i$$

where q_i is the query term weight of the ith term, and d_i is the document term weight.

In order to improve the model, evaluation is performed, which analyzes the user behavior and provides feedback to the ranking component indicating if the returned documents proved to be relevant. This task is similar to the feedback gathered in the recommender systems discussed in the previous section. However, explicit feedback rarely exists in the search case, as users don't typically leave ratings of the web pages such as reviews of the products in e-commerce scenarios.

As a quote from a 2006 CNN article says: "The Web, they say, is leaving the era of search and entering one of discovery. What's the difference? Search is what you do when you're looking for something. Discovery is when something wonderful that you didn't know existed, or didn't know how to ask for, finds you." O'Brien [2006]. This promise is still not fulfilled. On the contrary, oftentimes an accusation is raised that accessing the web via search engine creates a *bubble*. What we find in the search feed, is what is known about our preferences or what is popular throughout our network. It is difficult for new creative ideas to be found before they get some major traction. Fulfilling the vision of creating a search engine that would balance this and allow new ideas and content to be equally available is still ahead of us.

4.3   Ad-tech and RTB Algorithms

The ad-tech industry ecosystem is a highly distributed, cross-company big data architecture by itself and can be a great case study for building high load systems. The connections between the main players in this landscape

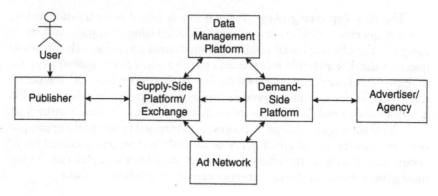

Figure 4.3   Ad-tech ecosystem.

are depicted in Figure 4.3. The main sub-system of the ad-tech landscape include:

- Demand-Side Platform (DSP) – responsible for spending advertiser budgets while optimizing campaign KPIs
- Sell-Side Platform (SSP) – which makes publishers' advertising space (inventory) available for sale
- Ad Exchange – facilitates the trade between the buy and sell side
- Ad Network – aggregates inventory and acts as an intermediary between a group of publishers and advertisers
- Data Management Platform – hosts cookie IDs and aggregates them into segments, while making it available to online targeting

A rich set of tasks can be found in the ad-tech industry, which require the use of very large amounts of data. In most cases time constraints play a crucial role, as ads needs to be served in real time, resulting in aggressive SLA for particular services. The most important ad-tech tasks include:

- Algorithms for Real Time Bidding (RTB)
- Dynamic Content Optimization (DCO)
- Forecasting
- Construction of cross-device graphs (see next section)

Real time bidding lies at the heart of the ad-tech industry. Let us start with describing the whole process and extracting its key elements. The steps of the real time bidding are shown in Figure 4.4.

When a user visits a web page an *ad request* is generated. An *ad exchange* sets up an auction and sends multiple *bid requests* to several *Demand Side Platforms*

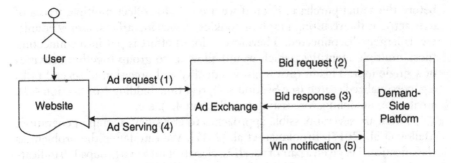

Figure 4.4   RTB message flow.

(DSPs), which participate in it by sending *bid responses*. After the auction is resolved a *win notice* is send to the winning DSP and an ad is served. Finally, a feedback about user behavior/feedback is collected (e.g. click, conversion, etc.). Wang et al. [2017a].

All of these steps need to happen very fast and requests are generated on a massive scale, creating the need for extremely scalable setups. On top of the on-line process described above, a number of off-line preparations need to take place. In particular, each DSP tries to optimize the campaigns it is running towards specific goals set by the clients. To accomplish this, machine learning algorithms are employed.

Let us assume we have a campaign which should be optimized towards viewability, meaning we want to serve ads to the users with the highest chance of actually seeing the ad. The Internet Advertising Bureau (IAB) defines a common standard, which defines what it takes to consider an ad as seen, which is more then 50% of the ad is in viewable area for at least 1 s. Based on historical data the DSP will build a model which should map available attributes of a user (e.g. IP, browser, visited tracking points, etc.) onto the probability of seeing the ad. Each time a new user generates a *bid request*, a model will return the probability value, which will be used to determine the price we are willing to pay in the auction.

For large scale DSPs, the dimensions of the training data sets can be huge, with millions of *bid requests* and thousands of attributes. This imposes constraints on the algorithms as well as computational infrastructures to execute them.

4.4   Cross-Device Graph Generation

In today's *omni-channel* marketing world, every user uses several devices and connects from various access points. Also the multitude of e-commerce vendors and sites stretches the customer journey across numerous services before the actual purchase. Even if we are able to collect multiple traces of user activity, the resulting graph of cookies, device identifiers, user accounts, etc. is largely disconnected. Therefore, a lot of effort is put into connecting those multiple identities, which would allow us to group together activities of a single user. This in turn improves quality and precision of several tasks e.g. personalized search (see Section 4.2), real time bidding (see Section 4.3), attribution modeling, forecasting (see Section 4.5), etc.

There are several possible approaches to cross-device graph generation. Malloy et al. [2017], Brookman et al. [2017]. We can define the problem as classification, i.e. given a pair of userIDs, classify it into two groups 1, 0 indicating that they are associated with the same user or different users. Tran [2016] proposes *ensembling learning* in which multiple algorithms are fed with the features. In this case neural network, extreme gradient boosting and random forest are used. The output of these classifiers are used as meta-features, which are treated with another instance of the xgboost algorithm.

In the same publication an alternative method, based on learning-to-rank, is discussed. Here the task is as follows: given a userID u, rank userID v based on the probability of referring to the same user. Algorithms such as LambdaRank, Burges et al. [2007], can be used to calculate the ranks.

The problem with practical application of accurate algorithms is the scale of real time data sets. For global companies providing, e.g. search or ad-tech services, the number of entry graph vertices exceeds billions. Some optimizations can be done with the use of domain knowledge, e.g. cookies from different continents/countries can be processed separately with minimal error. However, with the large number of features, the data sets can be huge.

4.5   Forecasting and Prediction Systems

Forecasting is a common data science task, which boils down to prediction of the future, based on historical data and any other available information. Most forecasting methods concentrate around time series data such as stock prices, temperature, system load, etc.

The typical real life time series data is an outcome of various factors. A higher level trend is usually affected by multiple cyclic and one-off events. To reflect this, Harvey and Peters [1990] propose the following model for time series:

$$y(t) = g(t) + s(t) + h(t) + \epsilon_t$$

where $g(t)$ is the trend function, $s(t)$ represents seasonality, and $h(t)$ stands for holidays. Additionally, ϵ_t is an error not covered by the model (we can make some assumptions about error distribution).

Several methods for solving the forecasting problem were proposed, ranging from regressions, through exponential smoothing, ARIMA to neural network models. Hyndman and Athanasopoulos [2018].

A regression model for the h-step ahead forecast can be constructed in the following way:

$$y_{t+h} = \beta_0 + \beta_1 x_{1,t} + \dots + \beta_k x_{k,t} + \epsilon_{t+h}$$

where y is the variable to be forecast and $x_1, \dots, x_k$ are the k predictor variables.

An important group of forecasting techniques is based on exponential smoothing. Holt [2004]. Forecasts produced using exponential smoothing methods are weighted averages of past observations, with the weights decaying exponentially as the observations get older:

$$\hat{y}_{T+1|T} = \alpha y_T + \alpha(1-\alpha)y_{T-1} + \alpha(1-\alpha)^2 y_{T-2} + \dots$$

where $0 \leq \alpha \leq 1$ is the smoothing parameter.

Yet another method for time series forecasting is Auto-Regressive Integrated Moving Average (ARIMA). Box et al. [2015].

$$y'_t = c + \phi_1 y'_{t-1} + \dots + \phi_p y'_{t-p} + \theta_1 \epsilon_{t-1} + \dots + \theta_q \epsilon_{t-q} + \epsilon$$

where p is the order of the autoregressive part, d is the degree of first differencing involved, and q is the order of the moving average part.

Real-life forecasting problems go way beyond classical time series and can involve, e.g. estimating values of certain variables over time periods. A typical scenario from the ad-tech domain can involve forecasting the number of impressions for a digital advertising campaign. Therefore, in this case we have to predict the number of occurrences of particular events in a given time frame. Such tasks require dedicated solutions and, in domains such as ad-tech, have to deal with huge data sets. Sometimes, the only feasible way of calculating such counts can be counting of past events matching a set of criteria. A bitmap model appropriate for such tasks will be described in Chapter 6.

4.6   Social Media Big Data

Social media big data has been embraced by several researchers as well as corporations as a key to understanding human behavior by measuring social phenomena on an unprecedented scale. Tufekci [2014]. The applications range from mood analysis, Golder and Macy [2011], through product or brand sentiment analysis, Goh et al. [2013], to disaster planning, response, and research.

Houston et al. [2015]. It is also an interdisciplinary field, which uses, among other tools, machine learning, natural language processing, graph analysis, semantic web, etc.

Bello-Orgaz et al. [2016], in their comprehensive overview of social media big data, enumerate the following typical computational tasks:

- Network analysis
- Community Detection
- Text analysis
- Information diffusion
- Information fusion

Network analysis deals with analyzing properties of graphs created from social media data. These graphs could be based on people relationships such as *friendship*, *followers*, or relations between content elements, e.g. *tweets (re-tweets)*, *posts (likes)*. As described in Chapter 3 on the sources of data, such graphs for largest global social networks can have billions of vertices and significantly more edges. A typical goal of the social network analysis is finding influencers, which technically translates to some centrality analysis. In Chapter 5, computational models such as Pregel or GraphLab will be presented, which are well suited and scalable enough to facilitate network analysis.

The problem of community detection in social networks can be mapped to some well known graph clustering tasks. Most relevant methods include finding connected components or cliques. The social media analysis has greatly influenced this field, to find most scalable algorithms for the age of big data and new measures relevant for the domain. An example can be introduction of *edge betweenness* as a new way of community detection. Girvan and Newman [2002]. Other measures, useful from a community detection perspective, include *modularity* and *random walks*.

By default, social media generates enormous amounts of unstructured text data. Therefore, text analysis and Natural Language Processing (NLP) techniques are at the core of social media big data. Unlike some other text corpora, social networks come with high number of abbreviations, slang, cross-language, *emoticons*, and other elements making it more difficult to process for traditional NLP algorithms. Typical tasks we want to perform with this data include:

- categorization
- topic detection

- similarity measurement
- emotion extraction
- entity extraction
- trend detection
- fake news detection

Information diffusion is another important phenomenon studied in social networks, which are particularly complex as they depend not only on static network topology, but are based on its dynamic, temporal behavior. Some techniques already presented in this book, such as time series analysis, can be applied. However, oftentimes we have to use more complex techniques such as multi-agent simulations in order to understand the evolution of information diffusion models. Gatti et al. [2013].

In order to get more relevant data, *information fusion* from multiple social networks often has to be performed. This is challenging, as different sources can have different structure, language, vocabulary, metric systems, or even whole taxonomies. One way of dealing with this heterogeneity is by use of semantic technologies. For example, ontologies are a powerful tool for aligning heterogeneous sources of data. Alignment on the topological level of social networks is another computationally intensive area. Mapping and connecting users across different graphs is both error prone and a resource consuming problem. Raad et al. [2010].

4.7 Anomaly and Fraud Detection

Anomaly detection has gained significant attention in recent years from both research and industry. This is due to several domains in which very large data sets are being generated together with growing complexity of the systems, which prohibits the possibility of enumerating upfront all non-normal scenarios. Examples of applications include network traffic monitoring (intrusion detection, botnet detection), fraud detection, sensor network management, medical diagnosis, and many others.

In most of the anomaly detection applications described above, all 4 Vs of big data, i.e. volume, variety, velocity, and veracity, are clearly visible. For example, in a real life network traffic monitoring scenario we will face huge data sets resulting from logging and monitoring of multiple sub-systems. This data will be received in near real time as various network events occur and in several cases will be incomplete or subject to error. At the same time we need the results in close to real time in order to act on the detected threats. Information about intrusion which is several hours old might be of little use to the attacked party, if the valuable information has already been stolen or some damage to the internal assets has been committed.

Intrusion Detection Systems (IDS) have been researched extensively and, to date, various approaches have been proposed. Peer-to-peer botnet detection is among the most difficult tasks in the domain. The attacks are distributed and change their behavior. Since the appearance of the *Nugache* botnet we observe adaptive behavior with a high degree of randomness. The whole Command and Control (C2) mechanism is highly distributed, with botnet nodes being connected only to a few members while being capable of coordinating network-wide attacks. Therefore, signature based methods have limited use as they are too weak to track changing patterns as well as being difficult to scale.

The complexities described above have led to the adoption of machine learning methods. In such a case, as the data sets usually have high variance, a lot of data needs to be gathered to fight over-fitting of the models. Singh et al. [2014]. A typical machine learning task in the case of IDS can be defined as labeling of network flow records as either trusted or suspicious. Other possible approaches include ontological models or hidden Markov models. Because of the focus of this book, it is worth mentioning that multi-agent systems have also been applied for IDS scenarios. Tsang and Kwong [2005], Dasgupta [1999].

Another big application of anomaly detection systems is related to data quality. Oftentimes anomalies in the data can indicate malfunction of some hardware or software components, which means that either some services have already degraded or we are potentially collecting erroneous data. This in turn can impact other services, which consume this data or skew analytics and decisions based on them. Such cases are of particular interest in domains such as telecommunication, Karatepe and Zeydan [2014], or sensor networks. Hayes and Capretz [2014].

For the problem of network anomaly detection we can distinguish five method classes, Karatepe and Zeydan [2014]: statistical-based, classification-based, clustering and outlier-based, soft computing-based, knowledge-based.

Statistical-based methods use parametric and non-parametric techniques to pick up anomalies without explicit knowledge of such events from the past. The downside is long training and complex tuning. The classification-based methods require training data, but are very flexible and can achieve high detection rates. Clustering methods on the other hand require no vast training sets, but require big attention to proximity measures. In the case of soft computing-based we can benefit from high adaptability, while scalability can be an issue. Finally, knowledge-based anomaly detection can benefit from human knowledge gathered in the form of rules, but are less likely to pick up cases, which have not been explicitly recorded before.

4.8 New Drug Discovery

Progress in sequencing and other biotechnologies has enabled creation of huge databases, which can be used to understand diseases and find better drugs to cure them. One of the important trends is a shift from symptom-based disease analysis towards more insightful molecular-based, taking into account DNA, RNA, protein, as well as environmental factors, Chen and Butte [2016].

The drug discovery process typically consists of the following phases:

- Understanding of disease process
- Target identification
- Lead compound discovery
- Indication discovery
- Identification of drug response biomarkers

Target identification is a data intensive process, which can be performed in various ways including: comparison of gene expression, somatic mutation, or genetic association data

Gene expression is one of the most widely used techniques. A single study can find differences in gene expression between disease and healthy samples. However, limiting oneself to one study can introduce bias on a biological, technological, or methodological level. Therefore, the greatest value comes from meta-analysis, which spans data sources and studies to find gene expression changes, which are consistently significant.

Somatic mutation analysis is based on finding genetic alterations caused by a disease. With cheap DNA sequencing at hand, large data sets are collected, which can be used to perform such analyses. For example huge databases of various cancer DNA have been collected giving better understanding on the mutations related to them.

Similar to mutations analysis, genetic association tries to identify DNA sequence variants, which contribute to various diseases. These genes in turn become targets for new drugs as well as indicators of risk levels for particular patients. In practical terms it is important to identify Single-Nucleotide Polymorphisms (SNPs), i.e. a variation in a single nucleotide that occurs at a specific position in the genome, which can cause different susceptibility to some disease.

Indication analysis is a process of selecting new or existing drugs for targeting a particular disease. The main data intensive techniques used to this end are: targeting of alterations, reverse drug-disease relationships for gene expression, drug–drug and disease–disease similarities, etc.

In most of the cases new drugs are effective only for some of the patients. Therefore, an additional element needed is identification of biomarkers for predicting drug response. This is once again a data intensive process. Typically it is based either on preclinical or clinical data.

4.9   Smart Grid Control and Monitoring

Over the last decades power consumption across the globe has increased significantly and will grow further. At the same time, a big shift towards renewable energy, has caused larger distribution of electricity generation. Adding more and more solar panels, wind turbines, geothermal generators, etc., becomes a challenge for the systems managing the grid.

The idea of a *smart grid* has been introduced, in order to solve the problems mentioned above. Introduction of distributed intelligent algorithms across the network gives us the possibility to monitor its performance in real time and react to unexpected events. Another term used to describe this new environment is the *Internet of Energy*.

In the general concept of the Internet of Energy there are a number of specific tasks, which can be identified. Jaradat et al. list the following challenges as the most important Jaradat et al. [2015], i.e.:

- Smart homes and smart city management – by utilizing numerous sensors located across either houses or whole cities, smart systems monitor electronic devices and appliances as well as predict future activities in order to optimize their functioning.

- Power lines monitoring – with the growing complexity of the grid, minimizing outages becomes more and more challenging. It is possible with the use of a distributed network of sensors to monitor grid components as well as the external (e.g. environmental) context. In the worst case of a blackout, the system should enable assessment of the situation and support execution of the restoration plan.

- Demand management – electricity demand is a variable, which is influenced by several seasonal as well as ad-hoc factors. Similar to general forecasting methods, a forecast needs to be made to adjust production and delivery accordingly (see also Section 3.5).

- Energy source integration – renewable energy generation is gaining importance, causing power sources to be more and more distributed and less predictable. Just as for demand side, described above, an accurate forecast is needed in order to balance the grid and take care of local shortage or excess of energy.

- Electrical vehicle integration – the growing number of electric vehicles can be used as energy storage. If scheduled smartly, this can help manage production peaks and act as a safety buffer for the whole system.

4.10   IoT and Big Data Applications

In Chapter 3 the way in which the IoT has created rich streams of data was discussed. This in turn opens a wide range of applications in domains such as healthcare and ambient assisted living, smart cities, smart homes, video surveillance, smart logistics and many, many others.

Video surveillance is one of the most computationally intensive tasks from those mentioned above. Not only does it rely on the heavy input of multimedia data, but requires the extraction of semantics and patterns from the original data stream. There are several sub-problems within the video surveillance domain. One is object tracking. For example, if a car starts being driven at a high speed across the city, police officers will want to follow it. Such tracking as the object moves at high speed, changing directions and potentially through heavy traffic can be a challenge with video streams coming from distributed cameras. A higher frame rate and resolution can improve precision of the task, but at the cost of even more streaming data hitting the system.

Another video surveillance task is suspicious pattern or anomaly detection. For example in security monitoring systems we would want to receive a warning if a person in a crowd behaves in a unnatural way. Humans can pick up such patterns, but with huge crowds gathered at mass events, computer-assisted security is crucial to prevent terrorism, theft, and other threats. Face recognition systems have made enormous progress and can support such scenarios, yet overall system complexity with hundreds of cameras and thousands of people can lead to a very challenging scale of computations.

Smart buildings are another scenario for IoT big data systems. Modern commercial buildings have a number of installations, from electricity, through water, air conditioning, elevators to the ethernet, everything is connected and interdependent. A number of major tasks for smart buildings can be identified which require fusion of data from several of the subsystems such as energy efficiency, security, emergency management, etc.

Optimization of energy efficiency is a very data intensive task. Firstly, the energy profile of the building needs to be understood and modeled. This can be achieved by gathering information from sensors located around the building. Once such a predictive model is in place, it is possible to forecast consumption given current configuration and environmental factors. This in turn leads to formulation of optimal strategies for long term energy savings. Moreno et al. [2016].

With sensor data it is usually important to maintain the order of measurements and to calculate various temporal properties of the physical quantities which we observe. We call such data time series.

Definition 1: Time series is an ordered sequence of values of a variable at equally spaced time intervals.

By $s[i]$ we will denote the value of stream s at timepoint i, where a timepoint is a time interval index. $s[i..j]$ will be the subsequence stream of stream s from timepoint i to j (inclusive). The stream with id m will be denoted as s^m.

We will further denote monitored statistics by $stat(s[i]^{m_1}, s[i]^{m_1}, \dots, s[i]^{m_k}, i \in [p, q])$.

Further we define useful timespans for calculating statistics

- Landmark window – when we calculate statistics between a specific landmark point and the present $stat(s, landmark(k))$ where $s[i], i >= k$
- Sliding window – with a given window size w we calculate statistics $stat(s, sliding(w))$ for subsequence $s[t - w - 1..t]$
- Damped window – when recent sliding windows are given more weight then the previous ones

In Zhu and Shasha [2002] the following statistics for data streams are proposed:

- Stream statistics, e.g. average, standard deviation, best fit slope
- Correlation coefficients
- Autocorrelation
- Beta – the sensitivity of the values of a stream s to the values of another stream r

CHAPTER 5

Cloud Computing

I n Chapter 2 we introduced cloud computing as one of major paradigms for building modern information systems. There is a strong rationale behind this trend. When *on premise* systems become overloaded and we enter the big data world, we need a means to scale with commodity hardware at hand or get external resources, which is what the Infrastructure as a Service (IaaS) cloud model provides.

Later in this chapter we will draw analogies between the cloud and multi-agent systems but also see how these technologies can work together in order to compose efficient platforms for information processing at scale.

5.1 Cloud Enabled Architectures

We will now dive deeper into cloud based architectures and the benefits they bring. In this chapter we will not distinguish transactional from analytical processing, assuming some abstract computational jobs are to be performed. More on specific computational models can be found in Chapter 6, where the IaaS cloud model can be applied. An in-depth review of big data analytics is located in Chapter 7. In the latter case also Platform as a Service (PaaS) and Software as a Service (SaaS) models can be applied if a cloud provider implements dedicated AI/ML capabilities.

5.1.1 Cloud Management Platforms

Regardless of the cloud model (Iaas, PaaS, SaaS, etc.), management of resources is not an easy task and requires specialized software called Cloud Management Platform (CMP). According to Gartner Gartner. CMPs are: *Integrated products that provide for the management of public, private and hybrid cloud environments. The minimum requirements to be included in this category are products that incorporate self-service interfaces, provision system images, enable metering and billing, and provide for some degree of workload optimization through established policies. More-advanced offerings may also integrate with external enterprise management systems, include service catalogs, support the configuration of storage and network resources, allow for enhanced resource management via service governors and provide advanced monitoring for improved "guest" performance and availability.*

Let us take those requirements apart. Self-service is nowadays an essential part of any broadly available IT service. Users expect the ability to order, reconfigure, and take down cloud infrastructure on-demand via a web interface, without intermediaries and without worrying about the need for lengthy activities like placing formal orders, etc.

In order to spin up new instances quickly, relevant images need to be kept ready. To this end, some form of an image service is needed, which is integrated with the computing infrastructure. When a user requests another instance, the image is retrieved and pushed to the selected computational node to be started.

As modern cloud services provide pay-as-you-go models, metering of all user activities and resulting resource allocation and use need to be kept. These events in turn can be processed by a billing service in order to calculate amounts for the invoices according to the agreed price list and the actual usage.

Typical big data applications are rarely static in terms of load and computational tasks. To secure adequate SLA, CMP needs to provide the means for real-time workload optimization. The users should be able to define certain policies for governing the level of KPIs, which needs to be kept, while keeping resource usage and the resulting cost under control.

On top of the core functionalities described above, CMSs usually provide a set of other features either natively or by enabling integration with third party software. These may include specialized storage services, advanced management of network resources, monitoring, dashboards, identity management, and several others.

5.1.1.1 OpenStack

One of the most popular cloud management platforms for the IaaS model is OpenStack. It facilitates efficient management of computer resources on which services and computations are run. The system creators also refer to it as the *cloud operating system*, arguing that it provides all major features of an OS on the cloud level.

The OpenStack map in Figure 5.1 shows the overall architecture of the system, with core functionality highlighted in bold font. Throughout the OpenStack architecture, the communication between the services is handled by the Advanced Message Queue Protocol (AMQP), which is an open standard application layer protocol, responsible for queuing and routing of messages in a publish-and-subscribe setup while providing reliability and

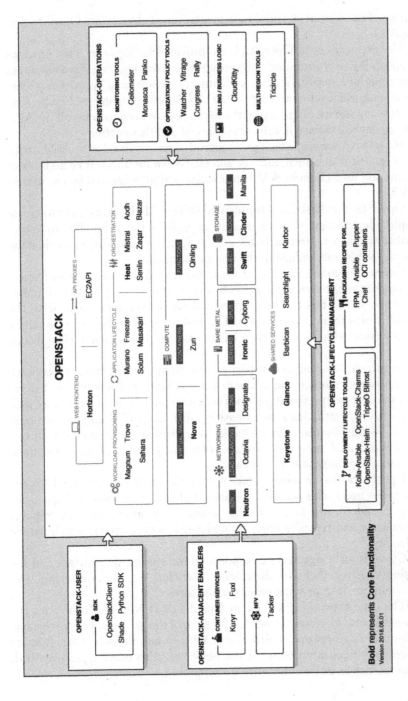

Figure 5.1 OpenStack Map

69

security. The current default implementation of AMQP in OpenStack is RabitMQ.

Identity services in OpenStack are provided by *Keystone*. This provides the possibility to cluster users into groups called *tenants*, who share resources (servers, storage, networks, etc.). Authentication is achieved by providing users with tokens, which allow access to other OpenStack components. Finally, *Keystone* acts as a service discovery, so the user does not need to know all the APIs upfront, but will receive it after after successful authentication.

Horizon is a service, which provides self-service web UI with dashboards. A user can use it to launch, manage and take down instances. It keeps track of sessions and uses OpenStackAPIs to execute actions triggered by the user in the UI.

OpenStack orchestration is provided by *Heat*. This allows users to create complex deployment with versioning as well as the possibility to create reusable templates. *Heat* includes also autoscaling capabilities, so that the deployed services can adjust to the current demand.

Ceilometer allows collection of the resource usage data across OpenStack. To a large extent, it uses information from events published via AMQP (mentioned above). To this end a dedicated *collector* reads the messages from the bus and stores them in a database. The main user of *Ceilometer* is usually a billing service, which needs usage data to calculate how much to charge each user.

As storage is an important part of any cloud infrastructure, OpenStack provides various storage types. The first one is *Swift*, which is an object store. From the user perspective it provides containers in which they can store data objects. Underneath, *Swift* uses a hashing structure called *Ring* to distribute data across the physical nodes. Thanks to replication, high level of fault tolerance is provided, however at the cost of *eventual consistency*. *Swift* is optimal for storing very large volumes of data.

OpenStack also provides a core service for block storage called *Cinder*. It provides users with access to *Volumes* and can use various storage technologies underneath. *Cinder* is best suited for storing data that requires performance and typically relies on dedicated storage arrays, which handle availability.

Glance is an image service responsible for storing disk images and for creating VMs together with the relevant metadata, e.g. size, ownership, etc. *Glance* can use *Swift* or some other storage service.

The core networking service in OpenStack is *Neutron*. It provides the dynamical network resources needed for each of the projects. The fundamental resource is a network, which allows VMs to talk to each other. Routers manage communication between the networks. Also other typical network resources such as Ports or Subnets are supported.

Nova is a service, which provides computer resources. It manages what instance types, with various computational power are used. It abstracts from the virtualization technique used, i.e. bare metal, VM, Linux containers, etc., so it does not need a hypervisor (virtual machine monitor, which creates and runs VMs) to be present. Recently, bare metal provisioning has been forked from Nova driver into a stand alone OpenStack project called *Ironic*.

All components of OpenStack can scale horizontally in a natural way by setting up multiple instances of that service. The situation is more complex with *Nova*, where two level scaling is available. The first one is classical horizontal scaling and the second involves creation of *compute cells* with its own database and a message broker. In this architecture there is one *API Cell* and multiple *compute cells*. The second level scaling is typically used for geographical distribution of services.

5.1.1.2 Containers

Containers are one of the ways of achieving operating-system-level virtualization, i.e. the existence of multiple isolated user-space instances. While the name has gained widespread adoption, mainly due to the popularity of Docker, other systems provide similar functionality under different names, e.g. Zones, Virtual Kernels, Jails, etc.

Containers allow developers to quickly create applications, which are broken down into components that can be deployed, tested, and updated independently from each other. It also allows the possibility to create a fully functional development environment, isolated from other application or system components.

Compared to VMs, containers do not need access to the hardware but rather abstract the operating system kernel. This requires less resources and provides big efficiency benefits. Also the modularity and scalability becomes easier. The evolution of deployment method from traditional through VM to containers is visualized in Figure 5.2.

5.1.1.3 Container Management

Similar to VMs, working with containers is most efficient with dedicated management software such as Docker. It works in a client–server model, with a deamon running on each of the nodes, responsible for managing local containers. Images for creation of new containers are taken from a central registry. Docker also supports scaling of containers over nodes as a *swarm service*.

While platforms such as Docker provide basic functionality for container management, as the scale of applications and the number of containers grow, managing them becomes a challenge. Kubernetes (K8s) is an open-source cluster manager software for deploying, running, and managing Docker containers at scale.

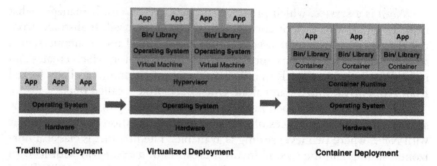

Figure 5.2 Deployment method evolution.
*Source. Kubernetes. September 2019. https://kubernetes.io/docs/concepts/overview/
what-is-kubernetes/. Licensed under CC BY 4.0.*

One of the main features that K8s brings to the *container* world are groups
of closely related *containers* called *pods*. *Pods* allow services to share resources
storage, network, etc. Because pods can be short-lived, service in K8s is a concept built on top of multiple pods. To the external world just one endpoint
is visible with a virtual IP. Underneath we can place load balancer routing
requests to pods, which can be created and destroyed as needed.

K8s architecture has one master node and a number of worker nodes.
The master node manages the whole cluster. It consists of:

- API Server – receives and put to action REST requests to the cluster
- etcd storage – provides persistence for the cluster state
- scheduler – automates several tasks such as new version rollout, recovery management, etc.
- controller-manager – takes care of controllers which keep the cluster
  in desired state, e.g. number of pods

A worker node is a place where pods are run. It communicates with the
master node and, based on this information, provides necessary resources to
the containers as well as manager communication between them. The particular components of a worker node are:

- Docker – downloads the images and starts containers
- kubelet – manages pods based on configuration received from master
- kube-proxy – acts as a network proxy and a load balancer for a service
  on a single worker node
- kubectl – command line tool to communicate with the API service

5.1.1.4 Container Management Versus CMPs

When thinking about the ideal architecture for a cloud computing environment, one can argue that VMs are an overhead which is no longer needed in the face of the possibility of using containers and modern container management platforms such as K8s, which can run on bare metal. However, VMs still have some benefit which should be taken into account. Firstly, they introduce an additional layer of security by separating the host OS from the guest OS. Also standard, well established and tested security tools and controls can be applied. Containers, on the other hand, leave some of the kernel resources outside its boundary. So if an application runs with superuser rights, it might be able to take control of the underlying system.

Similar to security of VMs, reliability can be controlled in a standard way. If the guest OS fails, it can be treated as any failing application by the host OS. Finally, as the number of containers is typically much larger then VMs, the resilience of such a system becomes more problematic to assure.

Given the above considerations, choosing containers or VMs is not a straightforward choice and detailed analysis should always take place. While choosing VMs comes at a cost of degraded performance, this cost can be estimated as just a few percent, which some organizations might be willing to pay.

The synergies between the two technologies go further, as not only does it make sense to run containers on OpenStack, but OpenStack on K8s as well. Nevertheless, the momentum is clearly with containers and this path has already dominated the main efforts towards the future architectures.

5.1.2 Efficient Cloud Computing

One of the most important aspects of running computations in the cloud is ensuring compliance with agreed SLAs, while minimizing resource usage. This is a difficult task to perform at scale. There are a number of internal factors that need to be taken into account, including the number and configuration of resources of various types as well as failures of software and hardware components. Similarly, the external world adds to the unpredictability by changing the number of users and the load on the systems, which can be predicted only to a certain extent.

Efficient cloud resource management can be achieved in several ways: spinning up and down instances of particular services, smart (re)location of VMs across infrastructure, load balancing of incoming requests across the cloud nodes. As these techniques are interdependent, ideally they should not be used separately but rather they should be combined by a single optimization strategy.

Automated scaling capabilities are nowadays a must-have component of each cloud IaaS platform. For example Amazon in its EC2 offering provides

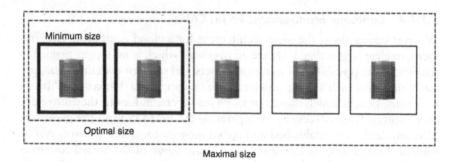

Figure 5.3   Auto scaling groups.

the *AutoScale* service, the role of which is to ensure that the user has the correct number of Amazon EC2 instances available to handle the load for his applications. Amazon [b]. It introduces the notion of auto scaling groups, which are collections of EC2 instances with defined minimum and maximum capacity limits. Within these limits the auto scaling functionality can automatically adjust the number of instances according to the predefined policies. The scaling groups concept is depicted in Figure 5.3. The scaling policies defined by the user can be either based on schedule or on specific conditions such as demand, occurrence of specific events, etc. Statistics and events can be taken from *CloudWatch* – the EC2 monitoring service.

Moving VMs between the nodes is an important capability, beneficial both in the case of optimizing efficiency as well as providing reliability. This process, called *live VM migration*, consists of multiple steps, Hwang et al. [2013]:

- Transfer initialization – confirmation of VM and target host.
- Memory transfer – migration of the VM memory state to the new host. This process is done iteratively, as the VM is not suspended and the state changes, so that a small portion of most recent changes is left for the final transfer.
- Suspend and migration of non-memory elements – at this point the VM operation is stopped. CPU, network, etc. are copied to the new host.
- Commit and new host activation – all remaining data is copied to the new host and the VM resumes operation in the target location. Network connection is redirected and the old copy of VM is removed.

Performing all of the above steps efficiently is crucial to minimize the downtime, which can be brought down to only tens of milliseconds. Clark et al. [2005].

Reconfiguration of network connections is a tricky part of the VM migration. One way to solve this issue is the use of DNS and performing lookups for the VM by their canonical name. In addition IP tunnels may be used if the machine migrates to a more distant network segment. Another option is to set up Virtual Private Networks (VPNs) for related resources.

Load balancing plays an important role in cloud computing optimization. Each time the load balancer receives a request, it needs to decide where to distribute it among the existing computational instances (typically VMs). This work is further supported by the underlying virtualization infrastructure which is responsible for atomic VM operations, i.e. multiplexing, suspension, resume, and life migration. Ghomi et al. [2017] identify seven categories of load balancing algorithms:

- Hadoop MapReduce load balancing category – MapReduce provides native load balancing and scheduling in a parallel cluster setup. More details on HDFS can be found in Section 5.1.3.1.

- Natural phenomena-based load balancing category – this is a wide group of algorithms inspired by properties of biological systems, e.g. Ant-Colony, Honey-Bee, or Genetic Algorithms.

- Agent-based load balancing category – see Section 5.2.

- General load balancing category – to this group belong algorithms such as FIFO, Min-Min, Throttled, etc.

- Application oriented load balancing –refers to a group of studies, where overall application performance is central to the load balancing task.

- Network-aware task scheduling and load balancing – algorithms in this group address the problem of network latency by modeling explicitly connection bandwidth.

- Workflow specific scheduling algorithms – authors of work in this group, look at the computational problems, where several tasks need to be completed, often with many dependencies between them, which put constraints on the computation schedule.

5.1.3 Distributed Storage Systems

In order to handle high loads in their systems, various cloud vendors have taken different approaches to building scalable cloud architectures. Kossmann et al. [2010] make a comprehensive comparison of alternative cloud computing architectures for database application from the OLTP perspective.

They start off with a *classic* multi-tier architecture as depicted in Figure 5.4 (classical). Client load is balanced between a set of Web/Application servers.

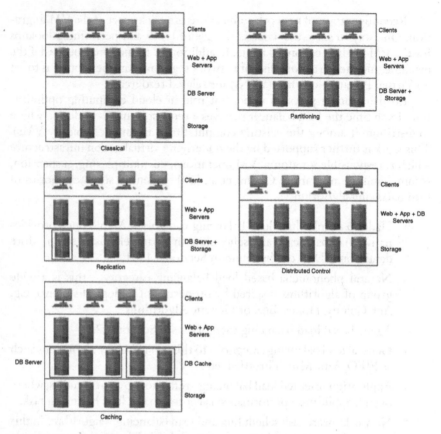

Figure 5.4   Distributed DB architectures.

The SQLs embedded in the applications are sent to the database server, which uses a storage system. While having many advantages, this architecture's big bottleneck is the database server.

Further the Kossmann paper shows how we can improve the *classic* architecture by using four different principles. The first one is based on *partitioning* of the database and controlling each partition with a separate database server, as shown in Figure 5.4 (partitioning). The architecture as described here is agnostic to the specific partitioning scheme used. This approach solves, to large extent, the bottleneck of the *classic* architecture. However, partitioning alone has limitations to flexible scalability as well as reliability of the system.

Another technique used to extend the *classic* architecture is *replication* (Figure 5.4 (replication)). Similar to partitioning, there are several database servers. In the case of replication, each maintains a copy of the database. Both techniques, *partitioning* and *replication*, can be successfully combined by replicating partitions instead of the entire database. This allows for better scalability as well as reliability of the system. The main shortcoming of *replication* is the overhead for keeping the replicas consistent.

A *distributed control* architecture moves the database servers away from the storage to the specific applications. The data is accessed concurrently, which introduces the need for synchronization of distributed read and write operations. This gives a great deal of scalability throughout the tiers, this, however, comes at the cost of strict consistency or availability in line the the CAP theorem described in Chapter 2. It is also possible to apply here the concepts of *partitioning* and *replication* described above.

The final concept for cloud database architectures is *caching*. As depicted in Figure 5.4 (caching), a cache is added, which stores the results of the database queries. Storing the cached data in memory allows for great speed up of reads. The main challenge here is maintaining the consistency of the cached data with the database. The concept of caching can be combined with all the other concepts described here.

Based on the concept described above, vendors have introduced a number of distributed storage systems, e.g. HDFS, S3, Bigtable, Hbase, PNUTS, Dynamo, Llama, etc. The following sections will describe a couple of them in more detail.

5.1.3.1   Distributed File Systems

A natural way of constructing a distributed storage is distribution of a file system. The concept of a Distributed File System (DFS) is very popular in cloud architectures, with the flagship project being open source HDFS (Hadoop Distributed File System). Such file systems are optimized towards storing huge data files. In order to support fault tolerance, data partitioning, and replication is introduced.

The Apache Hadoop project page, Apache [a], enumerates the following assumptions and goals of the HDFS architecture:

1. Hardware failure – in real life, on large scale hardware infrastructure, we can always expect some part of the system to fail. HDFS concentrates on quick detection of such situations and automatic recovery from them.
2. Streaming data access – applications running on HDFS consume huge amounts of data. Therefore, the focus is on optimizing high throughput rather then low latency.

3. Large data sets – HDFS is optimized to store very large data sets. The number of files should reach tens of millions and their size reach terabytes.

4. Simple coherency model – the general assumption is to write-once-read-many. This simplifies coherency and enables the high throughput described above.

5. Moving computation is cheaper than moving data – in order to reduce the network traffic, HDFS enables applications to move closer to the data they need to process. This feature is especially important with huge data sets.

6. Portability across heterogeneous hardware and software platforms – HDFS has an open design for portability across various platforms. It is written in Java and thus can run in any JVM environment.

The HDFS architecture is depicted in Figure 5.5. Each cluster has one NameNode, the purpose of which is to manage the file system and control access. The rest of the cluster consists of several DataNodes, which are responsible for managing the available storage. The file system namespace available to the user has a traditional hierarchical structure. Internally, the very large files are split into blocks stored in different DataNodes. The mapping of these blocks to the specific DataNodes is maintained by the NameNode. Each file

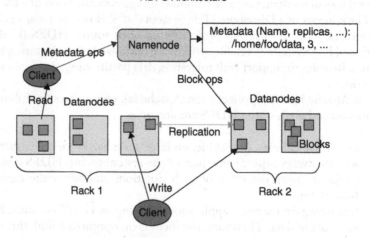

Figure 5.5   HDFS architecture.
Source: https://hadoop.apache.org/docs/r1.2.1/hdfs_design.html

system operation received by the NameNode results in a set of operations on blocks performed by DataNodes.

An important feature, which increases reliability of HDFS, is data replication. Each block is replicated according to the replication factor, which can be set at individual file level. During a write, the data is *pipelined*, i.e. it is sent to the first DataNode in chunks written to the disk and passed to the next DataNote, which should store the block and so on, till the last replica is created.

Smart placement of block replicas is key for achieving high reliability and performance. It should take into account several factors including physical rack setup. Constructing an optimal algorithm is not an easy task. For example, if we choose to store replicas on unique racks, we will achieve high reliability, in case of an entire rack going down, as well as fast reads. However, writing to multiple racks becomes more costly. Therefore, it is advisable to find middle ground between using few versus as many as possible racks. HDFS takes replica placement into account to optimize reads, always trying to read from the nearest data copy.

The HDFS metadata is distributed between the NameNode and DataNodes. The NameNode stores the namespace information as well as the transaction log. For efficiency the namespace and block mapping is kept in memory. The DataNodes keeps information on blocks stored in the local file system.

As described earlier in this section, HDFS is designed to deal with various failures. The most common situation is DataNode unavailability. This can be caused by network problems, node failure, storage corruption, etc. The NameNode marks such DataNode as unavailable and excludes it from further operations. Once a certain DataNode(s) becomes unavailable, replication factor of several partitions may drop below a desired threshold, resulting in the need for re-replication. Even if the replica balance is in order, HDFS may decide to rebalance the placement of blocks due to the current availability of disc space in the DataNodes.

The metadata stored by the NameNode remains the single point of failure in HDFS systems. In order to mitigate this risk, typically multiple copies of metadata files are stored. This allows recovery in case a particular copy becomes corrupted. The cost of such safety is an overhead related to synchronous writes to all metadata files, which in turn reduces the number of transactions per second.

5.1.3.2 Object Storage

Object storage was designed to hide the physical aspects such as files or blocks and instead abstract the data to the users as objects. Typically, objects in such storage are kept in buckets. There is some form of a simple REST API providing operations on the bucket level (create, remove) as well as on the object level (put, get delete, list). Objects are referred to by a unique key or name. Kurmus et al. [2011]. This contrasts with the traditional block storage, where we have an array of blocks addressed by index.

The concept of an object storage brings several benefits. Firstly, it is possible to enforce stronger security, as credentials can be checked at individual object level. Secondly, the concept of an object allows to encapsulate relevant meta-data in itself, saving the need for separate meta-data storage. Finally, operations on collections of objects, which are easy in object storage, are fundamental to several modern programming languages and algorithms. Factor et al. [2005]. In practice, object storage is often used as an alternative to Hadoop/HDFS to decouple storage from processing, allowing for greater flexibility and independent scalability for the two.

One of the most important implementations of cloud object storage is Amazon S3. Amazon [a]. It is a multi-purpose storage available through web service API. The S3 API is an open standard for object storage, followed by other systems including on-premise and open source solutions. Amazon provides a set of additional tools to facilitate easy administration of the cloud storage. This includes UI for bucket management as well as a set of REST APIs for both buckets and objects. A single object in Amazon S3 can reach the size of 5 TB.

Ceph is a free platform, which provides object, block, and file system storage in a single cluster Foundation. The underlying Reliable Autonomic Distributed Object Store (RADOS) can handle exabytes of data. Weil et al. [2007]. There are two types of daemon in a Ceph Storage Cluster: Ceph Monitor and Ceph Object Storage Devices (OSD) Daemon. There are several monitors kept at the same time in order to provide high availability. Monitors maintain the *cluster map*, which is used by the clients when they want to access the cluster. The *cluster map* consists of five sub-maps:

- The monitor map – the list of monitors and their properties
- The OSD map – the list of OSDs and their status
- The PG map – placement groups – algorithms for placing the data in the cluster
- The CRUSH map – list of storage devices
- The MDS map – metadata server information

The monitors use the consensus algorithm to align on the current state of the cluster.

OSDs are responsible for the actual storage and access to the data. Each piece of data is stored as an object, which is some file in a flat file system on a physical disk. For greater reliability, replicas of objects are created in the cluster.

To increase the availability and scalability, Ceph is designed without a central gateway. Clients talk directly to OSDs with the use of the CRUSH algorithm. Weil et al. [2006]. The goal of the algorithm is to calculate the location of objects in the cluster.

5.1.3.3 Bigtable (HBase)

A distributed file system, like HDFS described earlier in this section, is often not enough to serve the needs of advanced, data intensive services. Bigtable, Chang et al. [2008], is a distributed, highly scalable storage from Google, which has its open source implementations, e.g. HBase. The main abstraction in these systems is a sparse, distributed, persistent multi-dimensional sorted map:

$$(row : string, column : string, time : int64) \rightarrow string$$

Data in Bigtable is maintained in lexicographical order of row keys. To achieve partitioning, rows are divided into ranges called *tablets*. Therefore, for efficient data access it is crucial to choose row keys in a way which gives best locality, e.g. reversed URL notation (com.cnn.www). An important assumption is that each operation (read/write) under a given row key is atomic.

The convention for column key naming is *family:qualifier*, which allows for grouping of columns into families, which are compressed together. Column family is the level where access control, disk, and memory accounting is performed.

By storing timestamp, Bigtable allows storing different versions of data as it changes over the time dimension. For efficiency reasons, the data is stored in decreasing order, so that the most recent version can be read first. Also data retention is supported, by allowing specification of either recency of version or number of versions stored.

Bigtable is built on top of Google distributed file system (GFS) or HDFS in the case of Hbase. It uses SSTable file format, which is designed to store immutable ordered key-value maps. SSTable is indexed in order to find relevant blocks by in-memory binary search and access them with a single disk read. Lock service is provided by a distributed system called Chubby. It provides high availability by maintaining a master as well as replicas which can be used in case of a failure.

At the center of the Bigtable implementation there is a single master service. In addition it has several tablet servers and a client library. The master server governs the schema and handles any changes to it, e.g. new tables. It also manages the efficient assignment of tablets to the tablet servers and performs other administrative tasks related to file system maintenance, etc.

The master server handles only meta-data requests and the actual data operations go through the relevant tablet servers, which handle reads, writes, and maintain optimal split of tables into the tablets as the table grows. Tablet location is stored in a hierarchical architecture with the location of the root tablet stored in the Chubby lock service. The tablet location is also cached by the client library, so the metadata table is only accessed if the information has not been cached yet or is outdated.

5.1.3.4   *Amazon Dynamo – a highly available key-value store*

Dynamo, DeCandia et al. [2007], is an incrementally scalable, highly-available key-value storage system developed by Amazon for the needs of its services. It is designed to store objects which are relatively small and are arbitrary binary objects, so that no relational schema is needed. The interface to the data is simple and consists of two operations namely: *get*() and *put*().

To achieve scalability, the data is partitioned over a set of nodes, relying on a variant of consistent hashing. In this algorithm the output range of a hash function can be visualized as a fixed circular space or "ring." A number of *virtual nodes* in the system are mapped to a position in the ring by assignment of a random value. Key values of data items also get hashed and as a result each node is responsible for the region between it and its predecessor. This minimizes the effect of adding and removing of the nodes. Each *physical node* is responsible for a number of *virtual nodes* so that the load can be spread evenly across the system.

On top of this, data is replicated to provide sufficient availability according to the predefined replication factor N. As described above, each key value is assigned to a *virtual node* (called *coordinator*) via hash. The coordinator is responsible for replication of the data to $N - 1$ successor nodes in the ring.

Dynamo uses "softened" ACID principle, by providing *eventual consistency*. This is mitigated to some extent by data versioning, where Dynamo treats each modification as a new immutable version of the data. In most cases the latest version is the proper one, but when consistency problems occur we may deal with multiple version branches, which need to be reconciled by the client. Applications using Dynamo need to take this into account.

5.2   Agents and the Cloud

Now that we have reviewed modern cloud contemporary architectures, let us see how the notion of an agent fits into this picture. We will start by comparing the main concepts and paradigms behind both fields. Then we will see how agents can be practically applied to solve some of the tasks in a cloud environment. In particular we will review mobile agents as an alternative computation paradigm for distributed big data processing.

5.2.1 Multi-agent Versus Cloud Paradigms

Modern cloud computing environments, described in the above sections, represent the state-of-the-art approach to scalable, on-demand big data processing, which outperforms and overshadows with scale what has been achieved in other fields, including multi-agent systems. However, when we look closely at the main abstractions used in both worlds, we can identify several concepts, which have been present long before contemporary architectures were brought to life.

Firstly, following our line of thought initiated in the Introduction to this book, at the smallest level of granularity a single instance of a micro-service deployed in a container, resembles an actor or an agent as described in Chapter 2. It is an atomic entity, which can be brought to life, cloned, scaled back, and killed on demand. It has the capability and resources to cooperate with other related micro-services, while maintaining a certain level of independence, which allows it to operate in case of failure or unavailability of these external components. These features bring it close to the notion of an intelligent, autonomous, and proactive entity which we call an agent.

Secondly, collocation of micro-services into *containers*, *pods*, *VMs*, etc. is another concept present in the multi-agent world. Since the very beginning agent platforms were designed to host distributed entities scattered across multiple environments. For example, in JADE, Bellifemine et al. [1999], a concept of a *container* exists, even though its meaning is different than in *Docker* and closer to *pod*.

Finally, modern cloud architectures enable dynamic (re)distribution of computations across the infrastructure based on availability of resources, hardware failures, etc. This capability has also been present in the form of mobile agents, although explicit agent migration can also have different motivations such as other agent proximity, data availability, etc. Table 5.1 summarized the above comparison.

5.2.2 Agents in the Cloud

While we have compared cloud and agent paradigms, as adopting similar concepts to distributed computations, there are a number of opportunities

Table 5.1 Cloud computing versus multi-agent systems

Collection Property	Cloud	MAS
Building blocks	Services	Agents
Organization	Environments/Containers	VMs/PODs/Containers
Resource management	VM migration	Mobile agents

where these technologies can coexist and benefit from possible synergies. The properties of MAS such as autonomy, flexibility, collaborative intelligent behaviors, etc., fit well to the tasks needed in a cloud environment, where we expect autonomous management of distributed and dynamic computations and resources needed to perform them.

As described in Section 5.1.1 above, cloud management platforms provide various tools for automating the task of resource provisioning. Al-Ayyoub et al. [2015] propose to use agents for Dynamic Resource Provisioning and Monitoring (DRPM) system. The system constantly monitors the availability of resources (CPU, storage, network, etc.) as well as demand on the client side. This data is analyzed in real time in order to improve resource allocation and avoid both under- and over-provisioning of cloud resources. The system consists of one global and several local utility agents. Local agents are assigned to particular clients and perform local resource usage prediction based on historical data. This optimization task is not trivial, as it needs to take into account all of the tracked resources, while keeping the balance between ensuring SLA and reducing the waste from over-provisioning. The global agent collects data from local agents and based on this input, performs the overall provisioning. The DRPM introduces also a Host Fault Detection (HFD) algorithm for selection of VMs to be migrated in the case under- or over-provisioning. It takes into account which specific resource needs to be saved or scaled and schedules the most efficient migration.

In a different approach, De la Prieta et al. [2013] present +Cloud, a cloud platform managed by a multiagent system +Cloud covers three layers of cloud computing, namely IaaS, PaaS, and SaaS. According to a typical cloud setup, IaaS provides computational resources, load balancing, etc., PaaS – storage, identity, etc., while PaaS hosts management services as well as services deployed by the users. What is specific about +Cloud is the use of agents, grouped into organizations for specific tasks. Firstly, *resource organization*, which is distributed on hardware resources, consists of agents which are responsible for optimal provisioning. *Consumer organization* groups agents for monitoring of service SLAs. Finally, *management organization* takes care of management tasks such as supervision of the entire system, identity management, etc. Through experimental results, the authors show how this decentralized approach can lead to more flexible behavior compared to other centralized cloud management systems.

Agents have also been employed for the important task of load balancing in the cloud environments. Singh et al. [2015] propose the *autonomous agent based load balancing algorithm (A2LB)* to monitor and level the load on VMs throughout the infrastructure. The system consists of three types of agents: *load agents*, *channel agents*, and *migration agents*. A *load agent* is located in each data center and is responsible for calculation of the load on each VM. It maintains a structure called a *load fitness table* where it stores: VM id, memory and CPU utilization, fitness value, and load status. The *channel agent* coordinates policies for location and transfer of computations as well as initiates *channel agents* and collects information gathered by them. *Channel agents* are mobile agents, which migrate to a selected data center in order to assess suitability of resources available in this location and reports this data to the parent *channel agent*.

Whenever a VM fitness diverges from normal, a load balancing process is initiated. The local *load agent* informs the *channel agent*, which sends *migration agents* to other data centers. *Migration agents* find suitable VMs, which can be used for particular load balancing tasks and measure their load periodically. Once they are no longer needed they receive a self-destroy order and end their life.

In Wang et al. [2017b] a multi-agent system for energy minimization in cloud computing is presented. In this approach an agent is dispatched to each Physical Machine (PM) in the cluster. The allocation of VMs to PMs is decided based on an auction between the agents. There is an additional consolidation mechanism in order to optimize VM assignment to agents and avoid frequent VM migration, which is very energy costly.

While in this section we have mostly spoken about the use agents to perform tasks within cloud environments, the benefits can go also in the other direction, in the sense that we can use resources in the cloud to scale multi-agent systems. A few examples of such approaches have been described in the literature, e.g. Elastic JADE, Siddiqui et al. [2012], or cloud computing agent-based urban transportation systems. Li et al. [2011].

Mobile agents are capable of migration between the system nodes while maintaining their state and data. In the world of distributed data and the growing number of nodes ranging from data nodes to sensor nodes, this feature becomes particularly useful.

An example of agent application in cloud technology is support for the Open Cloud Computing Federation, which is a way to provide a uniform resource interface for the user. In Zhang and Zhang [2009] a MABOCCF (Mobile Agent Based Open Cloud Computing Federation) mechanism is proposed. A user's code is encapsulated in a mechanism called Travelling Bag, which is a part of a mobile agent. Agents are executed on MAPs (Mobile Agent Places), which run on VMs of the CCSPs (cloud computing service providers).

CHAPTER 6

Big Data Architectures

The changes described in the previous chapters, with regard to the data sources and shift of paradigms in IT system design, called for new architectures for data processing. Several such architectures were proposed both by researchers and industry practitioners. In this chapter we will start with the most common computation models applicable for processing large data sets mostly in the batch mode. A separate section will be devoted to stream processing, which at the time of writing of this book, is gaining enormous interest both from the research community and some major commercial vendors. Later in the chapter a combination of stream and real time data processing will be discussed. We will describe the Lambda architecture, which has has been widely adopted by the big data community. Further on, discussion of its limitations and alternatives will take place. Finally, some more specific architectures will be discussed.

6.1 Big Data Computation Models

Before jumping into the various big data architectures it is worth reviewing different computation models, which they allow to implement and run. To date several such models were introduced and understanding their differences is important.

6.1.1 MapReduce

MapReduce has been developed at Google, Dean and Ghemawat [2008], as part of the work on the Distributed File System (DFS), which finally led to the creation of Hadoop, where it became the default computation model. Currently the role of MapReduce is diminishing and more efficient solutions are replacing it but it is still widely used and serves as a reference and benchmark for other methods.

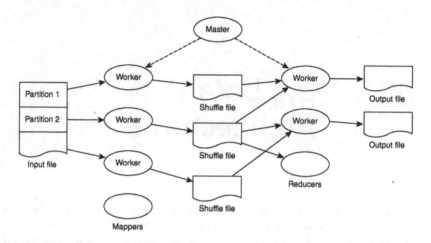

Figure 6.1   MapReduce

Figure 6.1 shows the flow of data in MapReduce. The algorithm consists of three phases:

- Map – generates a list of key-value pairs (k, v)
- Shuffle – distributes key-value pairs between machines, so that pairs with the same key k end up on the same machine
- Reduce – stores and performs computation on the received pairs

The simple and generic nature of MapReduce together with high parallelism allows it to be used for a wide variety of tasks, e.g. machine learning, clustering, graph computations, etc. Yet, not every task can be implemented easily in the MapReduce model. Its advantage is easy scalability over large data sets and with the use of commodity hardware.

Let us take a simple example of counting visits to different domains from a collection of atomic web page impression events. If we assume the events are stored in files distributed on a cluster such as the Hadoop Distributed File System (HDFS), the *Map* phase of the algorithm would locally create key-value pairs of the form domain-visit. This operation can be performed independently on each of the nodes. In the shuffle phase, the pairs with the same key (domain) would be transferred to the same node. The final *Reduce* phase will need only to add the visits for each domain and produce the final result.

The big disadvantage of the algorithm is the need to write the intermediate results to the storage, which can make computations much slower and reduce the gains from parallelism. Therefore, MapReduce is not suitable for processing of stream data. It also has the strict two-phase structure, which is not flexible enough for some types of computations.

MapReduce has also not been designed to handle operations on related data sets, such as relational joins. To facilitate those shortcomings, some extensions have been proposed such as *Map-Reduce-Merge*, *Map-Join-Reduce*, etc. *Map-Reduce-Merge* for example, maintains two groups of mappers and reducers working on different data sets and introduces a third phase called merge, which reads results from both respective groups and performs merge operation according to some implemented logic. Yang et al. [2007].

6.1.2 Directed Acyclic Graph Models

A number of computational models have been developed around the abstraction of a Directed Acyclic Graph (DAG). They mostly rely on mathematical foundations of formalisms such as *bulk synchronous parallel*. Valiant [1990]. We will now look at a few commercial and open source implementations of DAG.

6.1.2.1 Dryad

Dryad has been developed at Microsoft as a general-purpose distributed execution engine for coarse-grain data-parallel applications. Isard et al. [2007]. The computation process is modeled as a DAG. Each vertex is a computation and can be executed on separate cores or computers and in order to achieve concurrency. The execution graph can be modified on the runtime in order to improve efficiency and react to failures.

Compared to MapReduce Dryad allows an arbitrary number of inputs and outputs for each vertex. Graphs are constructed from simpler graphs with the use of predefined operations. For example a fork/join is shown in Figure 6.2.

Despite flexibility of Dryad and its ability to model complex computations, by 2011 Microsoft had decided it was not able to support its own big

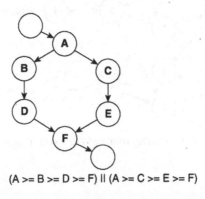

(A >= B >= D >= F) || (A >= C >= E >= F)

Figure 6.2   Graph operation in Dryad

data computation ecosystem and stopped the project in order to concentrate on the Apache Hadoop environment.

6.1.2.2 Pregel

Pregel was developed at Google to process large size graphs encountered in the Web (e.g. social media). Malewicz et al. [2010]. The computational model is expressed here as a directed graph, with user defined functions calculated in each vertex. The calculation is divided into so-called supersteps. Within each superstep the calculations run in parallel. Between the supersteps messages are received, values stored at vertices can be modified, and the graph topology can be modified. Figure 6.3 shows an example of computations where a minimum value in a strongly connected graph is found by message passing.

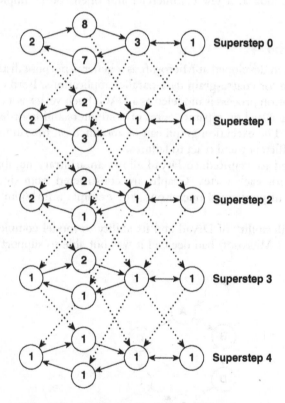

Figure 6.3   Finding minimal value with Pregel

An open source implementation has been derived from Pregel called Apache Giraph, which has been used for example by Facebook for some of its production data to process a trillion edges. Ching [2013].

6.1.2.3 GraphLab

Another non-MapReduce approach to big data processing is proposed in the GraphLab framework, Low et al. [2014], which exploits the sparse structure and common computational patterns of ML algorithms. It does not address fault-tolerance or parallel disk access like MapReduce and uses shared memory to store all the data. The idea behind GraphLab is to insulate users from the problems of synchronization, data races, and deadlocks by providing a high-level data representation.

The GraphLab data model consists of two parts: a directed data graph $G = (V, E)$ and a shared data table. The user can associate arbitrary blocks of data (or parameters) with each vertex and directed edge in G. GraphLab provides a shared data table (SDT) which is an associative map, $T[Key] \to Value$, between keys and arbitrary blocks of data.

There are two kinds of computation in GraphLab. Firstly, an *update function* can be defined to perform local computation. The application of the udpate function f to the vertex v as

$$D_{S_v} \leftarrow f(D_{S_v}, T)$$

where S_v is the neighborhood of v which consists of v, its adjacent edges (both inbound and outbound), and D_{S_v} is the data corresponding to the neighborhood S_v.

Secondly, a *sync mechanism* (Algorithm 1) allows definition of a global aggregation.

Algorithm 1: Sync Algorithm on k

---

begin

    $t \leftarrow r_k^{(0)}$

    for $v \in V$ **do**

        $t \leftarrow Fold_k(D_v, t)$

    $T[k] \leftarrow Apply_k(t)$

---

where

$$r_k^{(i+1)} \leftarrow Fold_k(D_v, r_k^{(i)})$$

$$T[k] \leftarrow Apply_k(r_k^{(|V|)})$$

Additionally, the $Merge_k$ function can be provided to perform reduction of a parallel tree to combine the results of multiple parallel folds.

$$r_k^i \leftarrow Merge_k(r_k^i, r_k^j)$$

6.1.3   All-Pairs

All-Pairs is a high-level abstraction designed for expressing data intensive workloads, which allows efficient execution of jobs submitted by non-experts. The simplest implementation of the All-Pairs problem is just a nested loop, see Algorithm 2.

Algorithm 2: All-Pairs

Input: set A, set B, function F

begin
    for i *in* A **do**
        for j *in* B **do**
             submit_job $F(i,j)$

However, the naive approach of running such jobs directly on large data sets usually leads to poor performance. A more sophisticated approach proposed in Moretti et al. [2008] allows greater performance for All-Pairs computations to be achieved. In the proposed approach four phases of the process can be distinguished: model the system, distribute the data, dispatch batch jobs, clean up the system.

In the first stage the system uses a model for estimation of turnaround time $T_{turnaround}$, which is calculated as a sum of data transfer T_{data}, time of computation $T_{compute}$ and dispatch latency. In the end the following equation is proposed:

$$T_{turnaroud} = \frac{(n+m)s}{B}log_2(b) + \frac{nm}{c}(D+ct)b + D(b-1)$$

where:

s – size of each element
m, n – number of elements in each set
t – typical runtime for each function call
B – bandwidth
D – dispatch latency
c – number of function calls
h – number of hosts

The hill climbing optimization method is used to estimate the best values for c and h.

For distributing the data a special *file distributor* component is used. It initiates the spanning tree of parallel transfers across the nodes. Authors show it is worth initiating additional redundant transfers to compensate for possible failures.

In the dispatching stage the abstraction allows monitoring of possible overloads as well as estimation of completion time. Finally, results are collected, checked, and the data can be deleted.

6.1.4 Very Large Bitmap Operations

Bitmap structures for efficient bitmap operations have been known for a long time. Traditional relational databases offer bitmap indexes, which were traditionally used for low-cardinality attributes, which have a small number of distinct values, e.g. color, sex, currency, etc. While being very efficient for multi-condition queries, if we have significant number of such attributes, bitmaps can occupy much memory. To tackle this issue compressed bitmaps have been introduced, e.g. in the form of run-length encoding (RLE).

As bitmaps find more and more applications in, e.g. search engines, forecasting, etc. they have entered the world of big data and needed further optimization. As of today, state of the art data structure and computational model for bitmaps are considered to be roaring bitmaps, which typically use less memory and allow for faster operations than alternative representations. Roaring bitmaps store 32-bit integers in a compact and efficient two-level indexing data structure. Dense chunks are stored using bitmaps; sparse chunks use packed arrays of 16-bit integers. Chambi et al. [2016].

Figure 6.4 shows an example of the list of: the first 1000 multiples of 62, all integers $[2^{16}, 2^{16} + 100)$, and all even numbers in $[2 * 2^{16}, 3 * 2^{16})$.

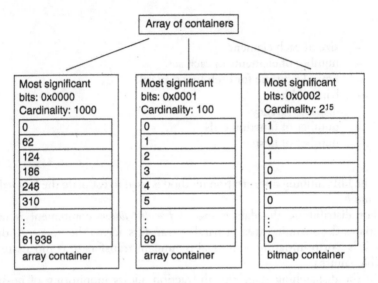

Figure 6.4   Roaring bitmaps.

6.1.5   Message Passing Interface

Message Passing Interface (MPI) is a standard for parallel computing, which comes from the High Performance Computing (HPC) community. Gropp et al. [1996]. MPI was designed for high scalability in distributed memory systems. On the other hand it does not have mechanisms for fault tolerance. While message passing between the processes was a typical way of implementing distributed computing, it was implemented in various ways. MPI brought a uniform interface that allowed portability of algorithms between the architectures.

One of the fundamental concepts of MPI is a *Communicator*, which connects groups of processes in the MPI session. Each process has a unique rank within a given *Communicator*. The rank is used to address messages send by the processes.

MPI provides point-to-point and collective communication. In order to support asynchronous communication, the MPI library should provide a message buffer. Collective communication can be of various types. Synchronization requires all group members to reach a predefined point of computation. *Broadcast* transfers some data to all processes. *Scatter* distributes an array of data, while *Gather* merges them into a single process. *Reduce* performs operations on the data received from other processes.

The basic operations described above can be assembled into more complex algorithms, which will be computed using the given physical parallel architecture. For example the pseudocode of Algorithm 3 would calculate Pi approximation by adding a given number of elements out of an infinite series.

Algorithm 3: MPI Pi Call

Input: SeriesLenght N

begin
> $Array\ A = [1..N]$
> $Double\ Pi = 0.0$
> $MPI\_Bcast(\&A, SeriesLength, MPI\_INT, 0, MPI\_COMM\_WORLD)$;
> **if** $myid! = 0$ **then**
> > $SeriesElement = CalcElement()$
>
> $MPI\_Reduce(\&SeriesElement, \&Pi, 1, MPI\_DOUBLE$
> $, MPI\_SUM, 0, MPI\_COMM\_WORLD)$;
> **if** $myid == 0$ **then**
> > $printf("Pi = " + Pi)$

6.1.6 Graphical Processing Unit Computing

Graphical Processing Units (GPUs) have been used for many years to render images, which is naturally a highly parallel process involving operations on matrices of data. As we have seen in Chapter 4 such operations are not uncommon in the big data world. Therefore, people decided to use GPU units to perform computations outside of the computer graphics field with great success. This trend is called General Purpose GPU (GPGPU).

In principle, GPUs enable execution of the same instructions over a very large set of elements in parallel. While CPUs are built for highest possible speed of each core and optimize instruction execution (e.g. speculative execution), GPUs don't provide this speed and sophistication on the single core level, but rather specialize in a high degree of concurrency.

The foundation for GPGPU is the stream programming model in which a *stream* is an ordered set of data of the same data type. Pharr and Fernando [2005]. In such a setup computations are operations on streams, e.g. copying. More complex operations are performed with the use of *kernels*, i.e. many-to-many operations on streams such as filtering, sorting, reducing (to one element), etc. Because kernels operate on entire streams, computations can be performed in parallel on a GPU leading to high degree of parallelism. Kernel based computation also requires little overhead for control of computation due to its simple *pipelined* nature.

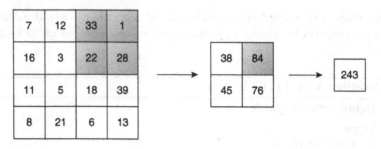

Figure 6.5   Summary reduction.

For example calculating the sum of elements in a matrix can be done as a sequence of parallel reduction operations. In each step the matrix gets smaller as parts of the matrix are analyzed and a single (sum) value is returned. The process continues until only one element remains (Figure 6.5).

As GPUs have been on the market for a long time, they are mass produced and are reasonably priced. For several tasks, which have high degree of arithmetic operation compared to the memory reads, this can turn out to be very attractive from performance and cost effectiveness perspectives. The two main frameworks for programming general purpose computing on GUP are OpenCL and CUDA.

OpenCL (Open Computing Language) is a framework backed by AMD, which allows computations to be not only on GPUs but also on CPUs, DPUs (Digital Signal Processors), or FPGAs (Field-Programmable Gate Arrays). Stone et al. [2010]. This heterogeneity of hardware, coming potentially from different vendors, calls for a unified parallel programming model, allowing engineers to concentrate on writing highly efficient algorithms. Indeed, OpenCL gives high level abstractions, by exposing the hardware accelerators as *computational devices* with its cores as *compute units*, which are further broken down into single *processing elements*. The OpenCL programming model requires creation of an application *context* and associates computational devices to it. After that Open-CL compilation functions compile the source code and *kernel functions* can be launched.

Compute Unified Device Architecture (CUDA) is a parallel computing platform created by NVIDIA. Ghorpade et al. [2012]. It relies on tight integration of CPU (host) and GPU (device). Parts of the computing run on the host are not parallel. Whenever an algorithm allows the same operations to be performed on an array of threads, it is sent to the GPUs, where a single *kernel* is executed at a time.

An important aspect of such a model is thread cooperation. CUDA supports this by the mechanism of *thread blocks*. Basically a thread array is partitioned and threads belonging to a single block can share data via shared memory, while threads in different blocks do not have such capability. This model is simple and allows high scalability.

6.2   Publish-Subscribe Systems

As we have seen consistently throughout this book, in real-life large scale big data systems, data flows in from various sources, in various formats, with high speed. Those circumstances make it very hard to maintain a tightly coupled connection between the sources and the processing infrastructure as well as internally between the big data system components.

Publish-subscribe systems were build to tackle this issue, by providing more loosely coupled methods for data transmission. This decoupling is realized by separating publication of new messages by the producers from the consumption by the consumers. To facilitate this process a broker (or a number of brokers) are placed in the middle. As not all messages are of interest to all consumers, they can subscribe with the brokers for the particular type of messages they want to receive.

One of the popular publish-subscribe systems is Apache RabbitMQ, which is a part of Apache Camel, an open-source integration framework. The messaging protocol in RabbitMQ is called Advanced Message Queuing Protocol (AMQP). It implements *exchanges*, which receive messages and distributes them to different queues based on predefined *bindings*. Each binding has a key, which helps the routing of messages.

There are four types of exchanges: direct, fanout, topic, and headers. A direct exchange is a default option, in which every new queue receives automatic binding to it. *Fanout exchanges* are used for broadcasting messages, as they send them to all bound queues. *Topic exchanges* route messages based on matching a pattern with a binding keys. Finally, the *headers exchange* is based on matching message header with a predefined value.

The Apache Kafka homepage advertises the tool as *a distributed streaming platform*. Apache [2019b]. This suggests more than just a publish-subscribe mechanism, which it was initially built for. Indeed, it is possible to use it for building real-time streaming applications. However, in reality it is probably the most popular publish-subscribe mechanism used in industry nowadays. Due to this fact, is has already been mentioned in this book several times.

The fundamental concept in Kafka architecture is *a topic*. Basically, a topic is a feed for publishing messages and to which multiple consumers can subscribe. Each topic is divided into *partitions*, which is an ordered, immutable sequence of records that is continually appended. Each record in a partition is

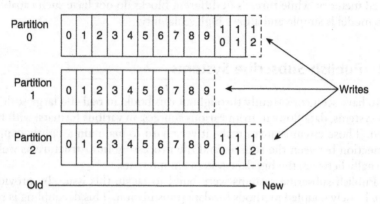

Figure 6.6   Kafka topic.
Source: https://kafka.apache.org/intro. Licensed under https://www.apache .org/licenses/License-2.0

uniquely identified by an identifier called *offset*. The structure of a Kafka topic is depicted in Figure 6.6.

Kafka is optimized to make the data in the topics available to multiple consumers independently at the same time. It only takes care of storing new messages and discarding the old ones depending on the predefined retention policy. The control of reading the data is on the consumer side. Each consumer has to remember the offset of the last record it read. This simple setup allows not only sequential processing but also moving the offset back in order to process historical data, which is sometimes very useful or even obligatory as we will see later in this chapter.

Four groups of APIs can be distinguished in Kafka:

- Producer API – used for record publishing
- Consumer API – used to consume the data
- Streams API – allows transformation of some topics into the new ones
- Connector API – connects Kafka topics to data systems or other applications

Kafka works as a cluster, where different partitions of a topic can be distributed over a number of nodes. For increased reliability, partitions are replicated, with one copy staying actively (*leader*) and other copies at standby (*followers*).

6.3   Stream Processing

So far we have discussed tools and architectures, where mostly batch processing took place. Recently a more and more important role in big data computations is played by real time analytics on streaming data. There are several use cases where stream processing has to be pushed to the extreme and a number of architectures have been proposed which concentrate on this issue. Examples of such applications include fraud prevention, intrusion detection, high frequency trading, etc.

The following key features of a stream processing system can be identified: ease of use, performance, fault-tolerance, scalability, correctness. Chen et al. [2016]. Stonebraker et al. [2005] proposes eight requirements for real-time data processing:

- keep the data moving
- query using SQL on streams (StreamSQL)
- handle stream imperfections
- generate predictable outcomes
- integrate stored and streaming data
- guarantee data safety and availability
- partition and scale applications automatically
- process and respond instantaneously

In the next section we will look at different approaches that try to implement these properties.

6.3.1   Information Flow Processing Concepts

Traditionally, before the big data era, the systems capable of processing large amounts of information flowing into the system from its subsystems, were called Information Flow Processing (IFP) engines. They differed from traditional systems, which first stored the information in DBMS only to process it later and as such were not able to return results in a timely manner. The systems designed to solve the IFP task fall into a few categories, such as Active Database Systems, Data Stream Processing, and Complex Event Processing (CEP). Cugola and Margara [2012].

Active database systems represent one of the earliest approaches to design systems, which can be applied to handle processing of large information flows. They are based on the concept of moving the ability to monitor and react to specific events into the database engine, rather then implementing this logic outside of it. To accomplish this, an active database must provide a knowledge model and an execution model. Paton and Díaz [1999]. The knowledge model is typically modeled in the form of rules describing which events, under what conditions, should result in a specific action. The execution model defines five phases of rule processing:

- signaling – event detection
- triggering – mapping event to relevant rules
- evaluation – verification of rule conditions
- scheduling – rule order resolution
- execution – execution of the schedule determined in the previous step i.e. the sequence of actions

Data stream processing is concerned with operations on the streams of data. The family of systems called Data Stream Management Systems (DSMS) has been developed to handle such tasks. DSMS, as opposed to DBMS (Database Management Systems) continuously process new data as well as the updates. Instead of traditional queries which have to be explicitly executed, DSMS provide so called *standing queries*, which have a longer lifetime and reflect instantly changes in the underlying data. Despite these differences, basic operations of relational algebra are still typically applied in both DBMS and DSMS environments in the form of wide use of SQL.

As an alternative to data stream processing, CEP systems are inspired by publish-subscribe systems and rely on distribution of events. These events are given semantics, which allows them to be filtered and combined into patterns. These patterns represent some higher-level concepts, which should in turn trigger some actions. For example a series of individual movement detection events can indicate an intrusion in the intrusion detection system and should raise an alarm.

As CEP systems typically have to deal with a large number of heterogeneous event sources, their architectures are also highly distributed. Usually they use a number of independent event brokers, which manage routing of the events between themselves.

There are two main approaches to the modeling of an event stream, deterministic and non-deterministic. In a deterministic event model, an event is a tuple of the form $e = <s, t>$, where s are content attributes describing the event and t stands for time attributes such as occurrence time, duration, etc. This model is generic enough to represent both basic source events as well as derived higher-level events.

In real life situations there is always some degree of uncertainty related to an event. It can result either from measurement error, such as a faulty sensor, or unreliable source. Also rules for complex event generation can be probabilistic. In such cases an event can be represented as $< e, p_e >$, where p_e stands for event probability.

CEP systems allow for queries to be submitted against the event streams. Various techniques can be used to match the incoming events with the patterns of complex events. Possible approaches include: non-deterministic finite automata, finite state machines, trees, graphs, and networks. Flouris et al. [2017].

In order to gain efficiency, the whole process of complex event processing can be distributed. For example the input event stream can be partitioned according to some criteria and sending them to different nodes.

6.3.2   Stream Processing Systems

After identifying major classes of stream processing systems and their properties we will now look at specific platforms which enable these ideas in practice. However, before looking at specific implementations it is worth defining the possible semantics for message processing, such as *at most once*, *at least once*, and *exactly once*, which are often confused and misunderstood.

In the *at most once* case we have the guarantee of each message being processed at most once through the streaming pipeline. Therefore, there is no mechanisms to retry the processing in case of a process failure or message lost.

The *at least once* approach introduces the possibility to reprocess an event in the case the processing is not completed successfully within the given time frame. However, we can have the situation when both the new message will be processed and the original process will recover and generate the result. Thus, more than one execution can occur, resulting in the duplication of data.

Finally, *exactly once* is the "holy grail" of stream processing. This basically means that whatever happens to the process in terms of failures with network or processing, we will end up with exactly one processing of the original message and thus with one output.

There are two popular approaches to the implementation of the *exactly once* functionality. One is based on state checkpointing, another on extending the *at least once* approach discussed above with a deduplication mechanism. The fist proposal is based on regular checkpointing of the state of the operators in the stream. If a failure is detected we can roll back to the last consistent checkpoint. The downside of such an approach is the need to pause the processing while restoring the state. Also the scalability is limited by the growing size of the snapshot.

The deduplication approach scales much better, however, it adds a small overhead to each message processing. It also does not require pausing of the whole topology for recovery. However, for the mechanism to process a very large number of messages, a sizable additional memory is needed.

Equipped with the knowledge of possible processing semantics, let us look at specific implementations of the streaming systems.

6.3.2.1   Spark (Structured) Streaming

While *Spark Structured Streaming* is the current stream processing engine within the Spark platform (see Section 6.4.1), we will begin by describing the old API called Spark Streaming. Apache [2019c]. The reason behind this detour is that firstly, it has been replaced only recently and several systems relying on Spark Streaming exists and secondly, it has a unique approach to process streaming data which is worth understanding both as a concept and as an evolution step in stream processing architectures progress.

Spark Streaming has been designed with openness in mind and as such allows the data to flow from various systems, be it publish-subscribe (e.g. Kafka), some storage such as HDFS, or TCP sockets. On the other end, the results of the processing can be sent to any other storage.

Traditional stream processing systems consist of several processing nodes, which perform continuous computations one record at a time. This approach has several drawbacks:

- slow recovery from failures of nodes
- difficulties in load balancing
- separation from batch processing

In contrast to the above approach, Spark Streaming introduced micro-batches, basically larger portions of data, which can be received in parallel and are stored in the node memory (see Figure 6.7). So rather than processing record-by-record, we have a second-by-second mode in which a micro batch can aggregate the events which flowed in during the last time interval. This allows for more flexible failure and load management. Micro-batches are also compatible with how data is ingested by the main Spark engine. This opens the possibility to use the features such as Machine Learning capabilities available in the platform to work on stream data.

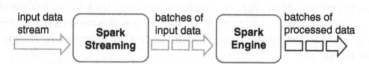

Figure 6.7   Spark Streaming flow.

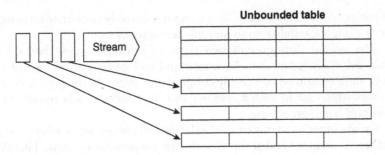

Figure 6.8   Unbounded table.

Spark Structured Streaming on the other hand is build on top of Spark-SQL (see Section 7.1.2). It shares the philosophy of its predecessor (Spark Streaming) by allowing computations to be expressed on streams in the same way as on batch data. Indeed, the same micro-batch mechanism can be found underneath. However, if we want to push the latencies to the extreme (single milliseconds), the latest versions of the system provide a new *continuous processing* mechanism which processes records one-by-one.

The Spark SQL engine takes care of the dynamic nature of the streaming data and updates the computation results as the new data arrives. In this sense analogies can be drawn to the DSMS systems and standing query mechanisms described earlier in this chapter. The useful concept to describe this mechanism is an *unbounded table* in which new data from the stream appear dynamically as new rows. The concept is depicted in Figure 6.8.

While Spark Structured Streaming provides very efficient in-memory computation, there is a checkpointing mechanism logging data to the disc periodically. Thanks to this end-to-end exactly-once fault-tolerance can be provided. Another important feature for tracking exactly-once constraint is adding offsets to the sources to track the current read position in the streams. This concept, borrowed from publish-subscribe systems such as Kafka, allows reading at the right place of the stream after recovery from the network or computation failure to be picked up.

There are a number of elementary operations on streams available, which include selection, projection, aggregations, window operations on event time, joins, etc., which can be combined to create complex stream processing logic.

6.3.2.2   Flink

Flink, which originated at Berlin's Technical University, is another data processing project from the Apache family. Apache [2019a]. Its headline is *Stateful*

Computations over Data Streams, as it guarantees exactly-once state consistency as well as high scalability up to multiple terabytes of state.

The system distinguishes two types of streams namely *bounded* and *unbounded*. Bounded streams have start and end given *a priori*, so that they can be fully consumed before any computation starts. As the ingestion order becomes irrelevant in such a case, we can treat such models equally to the traditional batch processing.

On the other hand, for an *unbounded* data stream we know where it starts, but there is no given end at the time the stream processing starts. Therefore, computations must be performed as soon as the data arrives as it is not possible to store the entire stream.

Flink provides mechanisms for both cases, so that *unbounded* streams can be processed in real time with the use of *DataStream API*, while *DataSet API* for *bounded* streams can perform computations in a batch manner, providing operations such as *iterate, map, reduce, join*, etc.

Within a Flink DataStream API there is a dedicated CEP library for detecting patterns in the event streams. It contains *Pattern API* for defining individual patterns, which can be later combined into complex pattern sequences. As opposed to Spark's micro-batches, Flink is using iterative transformations on collections. Since data elements are processed in real time as they arrive, it supports flexible window operations on streams. It also supports easy access to intermediate computation results.

For optimized performance, Flink is designed to perform mostly in-memory processing, using local disk storage only when necessary. Check-pointing of the state to the storage is performed asynchronously on a regular basis, in order to provide exactly-once consistency while minimizing overheads. Flink is highly scalable by working over a cluster of machines, which can be either stand-alone or run on one of the most popular resource managers such as Hadoop YARN, Kubernetes, etc. (see Chapter 5).

Figure 6.9 below depicts high-level Flink architecture.

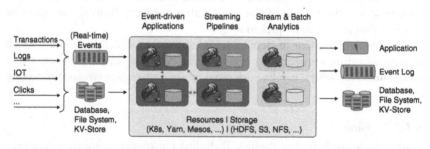

Figure 6.9   Flink architecture.

6.3.2.3 Storm

Storm has been developed by Nathan Martz and later acquired by Twitter where it was used to solve problems such as real-time query suggestion or spelling correction. Mishne et al. [2013]. Later on it was open-sourced and became a top-level Apache project.

In contrast to *jobs*, typical for batch processing clusters, Storm runs *topologies*, which are computation schemes in the form of graphs. Nodes in such graphs stand for computations and edges indicate data transfers between them. Apache [2019d].

The basic abstraction in Storm is a stream, which is a sequence of tuples (named lists of values). Storm assumes *unbounded* streams, i.e. streams that cannot be entirely consumed before the start of computations. A stream can be transformed into another stream by spouts and bolts. Spouts take some input, e.g. an API, and transform them into a stream. Therefore, they are the input components in Storm. Bolts implement further transformation on one or more streams like filtering, joins, computation of functions, etc. Storm topology is shown in Figure 6.10.

Nodes in Storm architecture run in parallel and can be scaled separately. Therefore, there can be several tasks in each spout and bolt as depicted in Figure 6.11. There is a dedicated grouping mechanism which tells Storm exactly which task should receive a given tuple.

Storm computing infrastructure is composed of a cluster with a master node and several worker nodes. The master distributes the code and tasks as

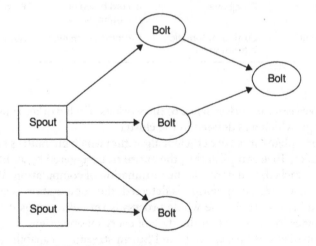

Figure 6.10   Storm topology.

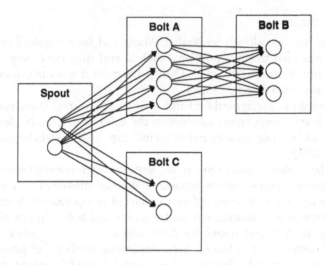

Figure 6.11   Storm task grouping.

Table 6.1   Spark versus Flink versus Storm

	Spark	Flink	Storm
Throughput	High	High	High
Deduplication	Yes	Yes	Yes
Comp. Model	Micro Batches	Streaming	Streaming
Window	Time based	Record based or custom	Record based
Memory mgmt.	Custom/Automatic (from v1.6)	Custom/Automatic	Automatic

well as supervises the performance of the workers. Each worker runs a part of the topology, which was defined in the cluster.

Storm implements a very efficient algorithm which guarantees processing of every tuple. To accomplish this, the entire tree triggered by an input tuple needs to be tracked, to determine the termination of computation. Whenever a timeout on a tuple computation is detected, the computation is considered as failed and is restarted. The whole process is very efficient as it need only about 20 bytes to keep track of the state of every message tuple.

A comparison of Spark, Flink, and Storm streaming capabilities is summarized in table 6.1.

6.3.2.4   Apache S4

Another example of a system dedicated to real time data stream processing from the Apache family is S4 developed originally as Yahoo!S4. Neumeyer et al. [2010]. While the system is no longer being actively developed we will go through its main features for comparison with other approaches.

The main purpose of the system was to process user feedback to search results in near real time. The S4 platform was inspired by the MapReduce model for batch processing and at the same time by the Actor model presented in more detail in Section 2.2 where it is compared with the Agent model.

In S4 events are defined as (K, A) where K and A are the tuple-valued keys and attributes respectively.

The platform consists of Processing Elements (PEs), which consume keyed data events and perform one of two actions. They either **emit** further events for other PEs or **publish** results.

Each PE accepts events of a specific type, keyed attributes and keyed attribute values. The platform must take care that a new instance of PE is created when a new value for a given keyed attribute appears. There are a number of standard PEs provided for count, aggregate, join, etc., which can be composed to accomplish more complex tasks. To optimize performance PEs should be removed when no events are received within a given period of time.

PE are run on Processing Nodes (PNs), which take care of the communication and distribution of events. A logical structure of a PN with its components is depicted in Figure 6.12.

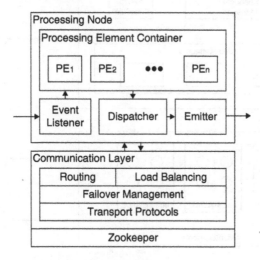

Figure 6.12   S4 processing node.

6.3.2.5 Mantis

Mantis is a stream processing service platform developed at Netflix, capable of processing millions of events per second and hundreds of parallel stream-processing jobs. Schmaus et al. [2016]. The goal was for Mantis to be "cloud native," i.e. abstract developers from cluster management, so everything runs in AWS. Furthermore, Apache Mezos was applied and a dedicated scheduling library Fenzo was build.

The architecture of the system is presented in Figure 6.13. It consists of the master and the agent clusters. Stream processing applications run as jobs on the agent cluster where workers are located. Three parts of a Mantis job are identified as:

- the source is responsible for fetching data from an external source
- one or more processing stages which are responsible for processing incoming event streams using high-order RxJava functions
- the sink to collect and output the processed data

On top of this a job chaining mechanism is available. It allows combining existing jobs into larger, more complex applications. Furthermore, autoscale

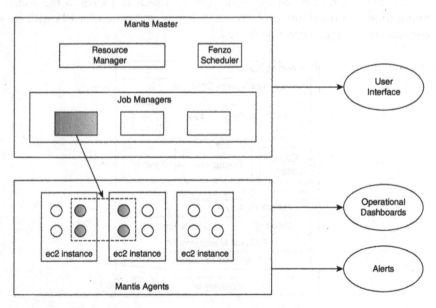

Figure 6.13 Mantis architecture.

functions work both on the cluster and job level to adapt allocated resources to the current demand. Other unique Mantis features include:

- job-level message guarantees
- seamless switch between push, pull, or mixed modes based on the type of data sources
- support a mix of long running perpetual analysis jobs along with user triggered short lived queries in a common cluster
- the ability to autoscale workers in a job based on resource consumption and the ability to scale the cluster as a whole

6.3.2.6 Other streaming systems

Several other approaches to processing of big data in real-time have also been proposed.

In Andrade et al. [2011] and Wu et al. [2007] System S, a large scale distributed data stream processing middleware developed at IBM T. J. Watson Research Center is presented. It supports structured as well as unstructured data stream processing and can be scaled to a large number of computer nodes. The main components of the system are:

- Dataflow Graph Manager (DGM): This determines stream connections among processing elements, and matches stream descriptions of output ports with the flow specifications of input ports.
- Data Fabric (DF): This is the distributed data transport component, comprising a set of daemons, one on each node supporting the system. It establishes the transport connections between processing elements and moves SDOs from producer PEs to consumer PEs.
- Resource Manager (RM): Determines the placement of processing elements. It also makes global resource decisions for processing elements and streams, based on runtime statistics collected from the DF daemons and the PE execution containers.
- PE Execution Container (PEC): Provides a runtime context and access to the System S middleware. It acts as a security barrier, preventing the user-written PE code from corrupting the System S middleware and other processing elements.

In Zhu and Shasha [2002] a framework for statistical monitoring of a very large number of data streams in real time has been described. This is useful for applications such as trading, where statistics of particular streams as well as correlations between them can be of interest.

The framework assumes a setup of K servers with N_S data streams. The computations are performed in two steps:

- Dividing N_S equally between K servers. Computations of single stream statistics.
- Finding correlated pairs based on the grid structure. Server X will read in its part, a set of cells S_X. Server X will also read a set of cells S'_X including cells adjacent to the boundary cells in S_X. Server X will report those stream pairs that are highly correlated within cells in S_X.

It is shown that an approximate algorithm for computing Discrete Fourier Transform (DFT) can be applied, which gives high computation performance with low error. Experiments were conducted on synthetic as well as real stock exchange data.

6.4   Higer Level Big Data Architectures

6.4.1   Spark

In the years leading to the publication of this book, Apache Spark, developed in the AMPLab at UC Berkeley, has gained a lot of momentum. Initially, this technology was regarded as yet another stream processing framework or as a building block for constructing more complex big data architectures (See Section 6.4.2 and later). Currently, Spark is considered by many as an environment by itself for efficient big data processing. It is backed by a large group of open source developers as well as some of the major corporations. A significant movement was the declaration by IBM to support the project. IBM called Spark "the future of enterprise data" and "the analytics operating system" and committed to training and development efforts.

While Spark can be regarded as just a tool for processing very large data sets, it provides a comprehensive framework which allows a complex system to be built without going outside its boundaries. Firstly, several diverse data formats can be supported such as relational, text, graphs, etc. Secondly, different data sources whether batch or streaming can be handled.

The Spark environment forms a cluster of machines, which allows for easy horizontal scaling. To manage the cluster it is possible to use Spark cluster manager or some other option such as Yarn or Mesos. Each application running on Spark needs a master node (*Driver Program*), where *Spark Context* is created. It connects to the worker nodes and initiates *executors*, that run the needed computations. Once the application completes the computation, the executors are terminated and resources can be released to the cluster manager.

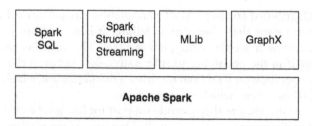

Figure 6.14   Spark stack.

The Spark stack is depicted in Figure 6.14. Apart from the Spark CORE API there are libraries extending the framework capabilities:

- Spark Structured Streaming – designed for real-time data processing based on the micro batches (see Section 6.3.2.1)
- Spark SQL – provides JDBC API for running SQL queries over Spark data, which allows the use of common SQL/BI tools
- Spark MLib – a machine learning library with many popular algorithms, e.g. regression, classification, clustering, etc.
- Spark GraphX – allowing the same data to be viewed both as collection and as graphs and performing computation on them

Spark was designed to overcome the shortcomings of the MapReduce schema. One of these limitations is that there is exactly one Map and one Reduce step in each computation cycle. So any particular computation case has to be converted into this pattern. Another limitation is that between the steps the data is written to the disk which slows the entire process. Not only is HDFS much slower than the memory, but the underlying replication process has to be completed.

In Spark it is possible to create complex workflows composed of multiple steps. The in-memory processing keeps the data available in RAM and on top of this allows it to be shared between multiple jobs. Only if the data does not fit in memory or when the final results are ready is the data written to the file system.

This solution is vulnerable to loss of data stored in memory if the computation process is interrupted. Yet, if the entire computation process is faster by an order of magnitude, we can risk rerunning the job from time to time.

The unique feature of Spark architecture is that it provides a unified engine for processing both batch and streaming data. This allows integration of batch and streaming processing, since each computation in a stream is working on a micro-batch. Originally, this common abstraction was RDD

(Resilient Distributed Dataset). As all computations are performed on RDDs, the resilience means that after a node failure, it is possible to recreate the lost computations from the computation plan. The distribution of RDD manifests itself in the possibility to split source data between the nodes. An elementary operation on RDD can be either a *transformation*, which generates another RDD or action, which returns a value.

RDDs are still used as they provide support for low level transformations as well as handle unstructured data well. However, since version 1.6 a new distributed collection of data called *Dataset* has been introduced. There are several more advantages of having a common abstraction in Spark. For example they can can be converted to *DataFrames* for querying with Spark SQL. A *DataFrame* is a *Dataset* organized into named columns. A more detailed description of SparkSQL can be found in Section 7.1. Similarly the MLib machine learning library can be applied easily to the data streams.

6.4.2 Lambda

An important approach at tackling the limitations of the CAP theorem was proposed by Nathan Marz [2011] in his blog. He points out that while we cannot get around the CAP limitations, we can try to isolate ourselves from its consequences. The idea is to hold immutable historical data separate from the latest updates, making both highly available and limiting the possible inconsistencies resulting from operations on mutable states. This architecture later came to be called the *Lambda architecture*. Marz and Warren [2015].

The *Lambda architecture* as shown in Figure 6.15 is composed of the following components:

- Batch layer – responsible for managing the master data set and for precomputation of batch views

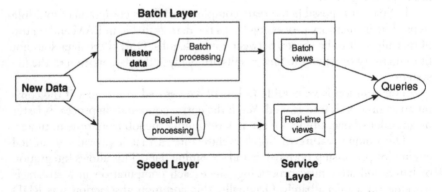

Figure 6.15   The lambda architecture.

- Serving layer – indexes the batch views for fast ad hoc queries
- Speed layer – serves only new data, which has not yet been processed by the batch layer

The batch layer is typically implemented with the use of Hadoop. It is responsible for storing the imputable master data set. Furthermore, with the use of the MapReduce algorithms it continuously computes views of this data available to the various applications.

The serving layer is responsible for serving the views computed by the batch layer. This process can be facilitated by additional indexing of the data in order to speed up the reads. An example of a typical technology used to do this job is Impala, which is easily integrated with Hadoop used in the batch layer.

Finally, the role of the speed layer is to compute, in real-time, the data that has just arrived and has not yet been processed by the batch layer. It serves this data in the form of real-time views, which are incremented as the new data arrives and can be used together with batch views for the complete view of the data. The time frame for events stored in the speed layer views can vary from seconds to minutes, depending on the needs.

The Lambda architecture is based on several assumptions: fault tolerance, support of ad hoc queries, scalability, extensibility. A key idea for the approach is the immutability of the master data set stored in the batch layer. The reason for doing this is to make it possible to make any kind of transformation or computation on the data we did not have implemented at the time of data collection. This also mitigates the cases when a bug in the software was found. After fixing it, we can redo the calculations for the entire history if necessary.

The general construction of the Lambda architecture does not imply which specific technologies should be used for its particular components. However, typically we can find Hadoop as the store for historical, raw data with MapReduce jobs for batch calculations, Storm or Spark for the speed layer, and technologies such as Impala for the serving layer. Speed layer makes frequent writes to the view, as opposed to the batch layer, it is more efficient to store them in a database such as HBase or Cassandra.

6.4.3 Multi-Agent View of the Lambda Architecture

The *Lambda architecture* for processing big data, described in section 6.4.2, can be transformed into a multi-agent system. Twardowski and Ryżko [2014]. Agents take responsibility for the communication between the three main architecture components. To this end they are typically used for MAS passing of asynchronous messages.

As in the original *Lambda architecture*, the *batch layer* is responsible for running batch jobs, which result in *batch views*, *real-time views* are filled by the *speed layer*, and the *service layer* picks both of those outputs for supplying business applications.

Agents come in as facilitators of this process. Input data streams are handled by dedicated *stream receiver agents*, which are responsible for simple data pre-processing, for example filtering, formatting, serialization, etc. The role of the *archiver agent* is to pick the data from the *stream receiver agent* and write it to the *batch layer* storage, e.g. HDFS. Batch jobs are run according to the schedule and are handled by *batch driver agent*, which coordinates those computations and *batch worker agents*, which handle the actual work for a given piece of data. The results of jobs are stored in the relevant *batch views*.

The *stream processing agent* is in control of handling new data in the speed layer. It receives the same stream of data as the *stream receiver agent*, but rather than just putting it into storage it pushes it for direct processing. This is the job of *real-time worker agents*, which perform the chain of real time computations on the constantly flowing stream of data. The results of those tasks are visible in the *real-time views*, which get updated on a regular basis and are stored in memory for efficiency reasons.

The *service agent's* role is to provide business applications with the relevant data from the *batch views* and *real-time views*. The architecture assumes multiple types of *service agents* created for each application and unique instances created for each session. To accomplish it's task, the *service agent* calls *aggregator agents* on both the batch and speed sides in order to access the data, who query the views and perform necessary transformation.

Figure 6.16 presents the Lambda architecture for big data processing using multi-agent systems.

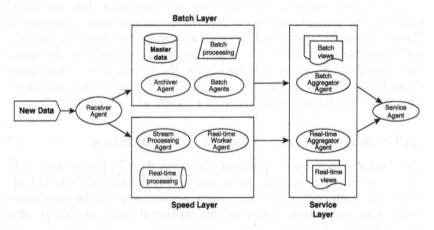

Figure 6.16   Architecture for multi-agent big data processing.

Applying agents in each system component allows for the uniform communication between them. This also can be extended to the outside world. If we wish to create more specialized agents around the main data processing infrastructure, e.g. located somewhere in the IoT environment, we can integrate them easily and they can become both suppliers and consumers of the data flowing through the pipelines.

6.4.4 Questioning the Lambda

As one of the shortcomings of the Lambda architecture described in the previous section, it is pointed out the code to process the data has to be maintained in two layers, i.e. batch layer and speed Layer for offline and online processing. Both of the layers are usually implemented with different technologies, so the code has to be synchronized between them.

One of the approaches to tackle this issue is to have a common code base for the two layers by using common libraries or introducing some kind of abstraction shared between the flows. Examples of such frameworks are Summingbird or Lambdoop. Casado [2013]. While this can save some effort, maintenance of the two layers is still an overhead that needs to be taken care of.

It can be argued that with the improvement of the technologies surrounding Hadoop, the speed layer is in many applications not necessary. If we shorten the batch cycles, the latency in data availability can be reduced. On the other hand new faster tools for accessing the data stored on Hadoop, such as Impala, Drill, or new versions of Tez, etc., make it possible to take some actions on the data in a reasonable time.

Another approach is to give up the batch layer altogether and process everything in the speed layer. An example of such an architecture, called Kappa Kreps, proposes that incoming data be processed in streaming and whenever a larger history is needed, it can be restreamed from Kafka buffers, or if we have to go back even further, from the historical data cluster (if there is one).

The flow of data in the Kappa architecture is shown in Figure 6.17. The assumption is that when we want to reprocess old data, due to a new algorithm version, a bug, etc., we start a new instance in streaming, starting at the latest point in history which makes sense from the business application needs. The result of this processing will feed a new table in the serving DB. Once all the data is processed we switch the tables, so that the new data becomes the source for the production systems or analytics.

Yet another approach to handling doubts about having two separate processing layers is introduced in the Delta architecture. The flow of data in this setup is shown in Figure 6.18. The idea is to use Kafka for additional

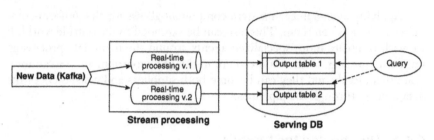

Figure 6.17   Kappa architecture.

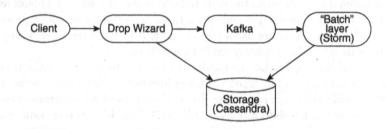

Figure 6.18   Delta architecture.

persistence, which will eventually process the data incrementally via Storm, that has taken the place of Hadoop Batch layer O'Neill.

6.5   Industry and Other Approaches

In Pääkkönen and Pakkala [2015] a technology independent reference architecture for big data is presented based on a number of industry-wide implementations. The related technologies, products, and services have been classified in accordance with the presented architecture.

Further, in the cited paper the authors map the use cases (Facebook, Linkedin, Twitter, Netflix, etc.) onto the presented reference architecture.

The authors conclude, that it was possible to construct the architecture by means of inductive reasoning from industrial use cases. This is further proved by mapping of the individual examples onto the reference architecture. The study, while staying on a very high level of abstraction, is a useful summary of best practice examples and for analyzing analogies and differences between various approaches.

The architecture of real time data processing at Facebook has been presented in Chen et al. [2016]. The main assumption behind the work was to

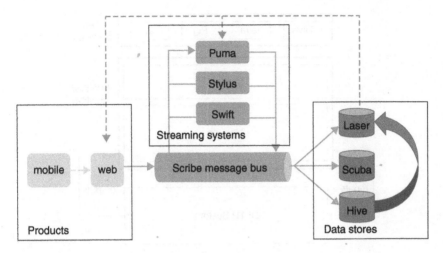

Figure 6.19   Realtime data processing at Facebook.

decouple the data transport mechanism from the processing, which allows for higher scalability and fault tolerance. The few second latency resulting from such a setup is acceptable for the applications of this architecture, e.g. aggregated voice of people, mobile analytics, dashboard queries, etc.

Figure 6.19 shows the overview of the system involved in big data processing. Scribe is a persistent, distributed messaging system. It is responsible for collecting, aggregating, and delivering high volumes of log data to real-time and batch systems with a few seconds of latency and high throughput. Similar to Kafka *topics* Scribe has *categories*, i.e. a specific stream of data where each time a write or read is performed. The data is further partitioned into buckets, which can be processed in parallel. Persistence is provided in the form of writing data to the HDFS storage.

Puma is a stream processing system, which provides pre-computed query results for simple aggregation queries. It also provides filtering and processing of Scribe streams. Puma applications are written in a SQL-like language. Java UDFs (User-Defined Functions) can be added. In general Puma is optimized for compiled queries rather than ad-hoc analysis.

Stylus is a low-level stream processing framework written in C++, which reads from one Scribe stream and writes to another stream or some data store. The processing can be a complex DAG consisting of simple stateful or stateless processors.

Swift is a basic stream processing engine. It allows checkpointing for Scribe, so that when an app fails, it is possible to restart from the last checkpoint. Apps can communicate with Swift via system-level pipes.

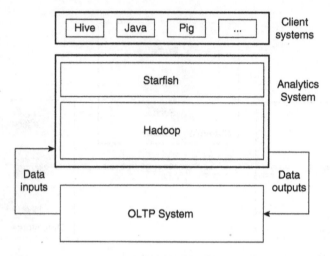

Figure 6.20   Starfish ecosystem

A self-tuning big data analytics system called Starfish was build by researchers at the Duke University. Herodotou et al. [2011]. The goal is to provide optimization while covering the technical details of the Hadoop platform from users who do not have the know how to go down to the level of elementary system parameters. The location of Starfish in the Hadoop ecosystem is depicted in Figure 6.20.

Three levels at which the system performs tuning are:

- job-level tuning – optimizes tens of parameters which influence the performance of MapReduce jobs on Hadoop
- workflow-level tuning – works on efficient scheduling of jobs
- workload-level tuning
  - data-flow sharing
  - materialization
  - reorganization

6.6   Actor and Agent-Based Big Data Architectures

An example of an actor-like model for big data processing is presented in Jiang et al. [2014]. The epic system was designed to handle the variety out of the big data 3V (Volume, Velocity, Variety). To handle this variety extensions can be defined, which are dedicated for specific data type and map the the data model onto epiC concurrent model. The paper presents two data processing models namely MapReduce and the relational model.

The main contribution claimed by the authors is the creation of a single computation environment, with a common runtime layer and allowing for specific communication patters via a plug-in system. The core for concurrent programming is designed in an actor-like model, i.e. it consists of independent computations coordinated by message passing.

The elementary computation entity in epiC is called *unit*. It operates in the following steps:

- activation on receiving a message
- loading data from the storage
- processing the data
- writing results to storage
- sending message to the master network

The master network aggregates a number of masters which provide:

- naming service – manages two-level namespace, with the grouping level for units with common code and individual unit level
- message service – with load balancing by multiple masters and replication functionalities
- schedule service – allowing for monitoring and restarting of units if a failure is detected

A similar concept has been proposed by Wang et al. [2010] in the Transformer framework. It is based on two primitives *send( )* and *receive( )*. To demonstrate the usability of the approach, three programming models were implemented namely Dryad-like data flow, MapReduce, and All-Pairs.

The framework is divided into two parts. The common runtime system implements the two most common operations, i.e. execution of a task on a machine and transfer of data between machines. Model specific layer users *send()* and *receive()* of the runtime to implement a specific computation model. As far as fault tolerance is concerned, the runtime layers can detect the node or data transfer failure but the recovery has to be done by the model specific layer.

In Transformer two types of nodes are distinguished, namely *master* and *slaves*. The master is responsible for message dispatching and monitoring of the slaves. The slave nodes have a supervisor, which further dispatches the messages to the specific components.

CHAPTER 7

Big Data Analytics, Mining, and Machine Learning

One of the main goals of efficient big data processing is performing some sort of analytics, which useful insights to be gained about the data and making it actionable from the business perspective. Typically, three types of analytics can be distinguished:

- Descriptive – allows you to summarize and understand what has happened based on the available data
- Predictive – makes predictions about the future taking into account past events
- Prescriptive – helps to make the best out of possible actions in order to achieve the desired outcome

Advances in parallel computing architectures and computational models, make it attractive to consider distribution of ML-DM (Machine Learning–Data Mining) algorithms. Taking into account the explicit distribution of the data resources, decentralization of computations often becomes obligatory. Yet, not all algorithms can be distributed in a straightforward way. Ghoting et al. [2011].

Firstly, taking a sequential algorithm and throwing it into a generic parallelization framework, typically creates a lot of trouble with communication and data management. So ideally dedicated versions of the algorithms should be implemented. On the other hand, the researchers would like to be able to code in an easy way, which they are used to.

Secondly, the specifics of ML-DM require several interactions and prototyping. Often a wide variety of algorithms need to be tried. Rapid prototyping in a distributed environment is not easy. Ideally, early phases would be done on a workstation, moving seamlessly to a cluster for large scale experiments.

Finally, there is a gap between building generic purpose parallelization, optimized for low level parallel computation models and domain specific requirements, which can vary depending on the sub-domain of ML-DM, which is used in a particular case. Regression models require different atomic operations that graph models or deep learning models and it may even be most optimal to run them on different hardware (CPU/GPU).

All of these challenges make creation of a universal big data ML environment far from obvious. In this chapter we will review different approaches and platforms proposed in the research and industry.

Building on the knowledge of the architectures described in the previous chapters, we will now dive into the world of analytics starting from the classical SQL access to data and then moving further towards building complex statistical or machine learning models.

7.1   To SQL or Not to SQL

In Chapter 2 we discussed how database paradigms evolved, leading to the current situation, when more and more data is stored in formats other then relational databases. As NoSQL storage started to be widely used for building services, Hadoop clusters started holding main enterprise data assets, streaming systems started pumping data from the Internet and smart devices, we experience a wide variety of formats and consequently various data access methods and protocols.

Yet, SQL is still regarded as the analytics *lingua franca*, regardless of the underlying data storage model. Whether it's exploratory data analysis, ad-hoc queries, reporting, or dashboards, SQL interface is a must-have feature users expect.

One of the reasons for this, is that a very big number of the data sets are still available in the legacy systems and their relational databases. Similarly, classical data warehouses are still the central analytical hubs for several companies. There is also a huge skills gap between the abilities of a typical business analyst, who has a great domain experience and potentially some statistical background, and the technological fluency needed to navigate in the modern big data stack, such as creating native Hadoop or Spark jobs, even if it does not involve programming *sensu stricto*.

To be able to blend within the legacy environments, new modern big data frameworks need to implement SQL interfaces, in order to connect with other systems and existing analytical front end tools. This obligation of including SQL or some SQL-like interface within big data tools, comes at a price of merging technologies from two different worlds, which often ends in questionable results as far as the functionality or performance are concerned.

In practice oftentimes an SQL interface, which is in early development stage, does not give required functionality (e.g. all analytical functions) or lacks desired performance. The alternative of involving the engineers, who are able to implement the native job for data processing, makes the process longer and increases the loop between the iterations, which are often needed in analytical work. Also change management becomes problematic and inefficient.

The above gaps put pressure on modern big data analytical environments, to bridge them by bringing unstructured distributed data to the users in the most efficient way. We will review in the following section how it has been addressed by various frameworks.

7.1.1   SQL Hadoop Interfaces

With Hadoop becoming the primary storage for largest data sets in several organizations, giving SQL access to this environment is in high demand from the users responsible for analytics. Not surprisingly a large number of open source and commercial products have been developed for this task. The most important include Hive, Spark SQL, Impala, Drill, Presto, IBM Big SQL, etc.

The evolution of Hive architecture is a good example of how the approaches to efficient SQL-on-Hadoop changed over time. In the early attempts, Hive relied on the MapReduce computational schema described in Section 6.1.1. Figure 7.1 shows the major components of this architecture.

Such an approach is elegant, since it transforms any SQL statement into the computational schema, which is native to the Hadoop environment. It is therefore possible to take advantage of all the features of this environment such as scalability and fault tolerance. However, as discussed in the previous

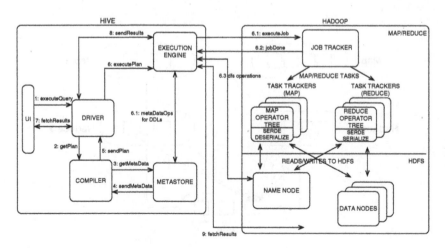

Figure 7.1   Hive architecture (MapReduce)

chapter, MapReduce has a number of drawbacks, such as a strict map-reduce pattern or frequent writes of the intermediate results to the disk, which limit its performance capabilities. While these limitations can be acceptable for a certain class of batch tasks, ad-hoc analytics requires a reasonable response time for queries as it is an interactive working model.

Due to performance issues, in the later versions of Hive a new execution engine called Tez was introduced. To a large extent it was inspired by the Dryad framework (described in Section 6.1.2.1), i.e. execution of processing tasks forming a directed acyclic graph. The main idea was to skip writing the data to the disk and pass it directly between computation steps. Figure 7.2 shows a sample query broken down into the elementary operations.

SQL has been built directly on relational paradigms. Therefore, apart from comparing alignment with SQL standards, the main concern with the above frameworks is their performance when processing very large data sets. Several attempts to perform objective benchmarks have been made. In Floratou et al. [2014] researchers from IBM compare Hive and Impala. As mentioned above, Hive is a native Hadoop SQL interface utilizing underlying MapReduce or Tez mechanism. On the other hand Impala is built on the concept of shared-nothing parallel database mechanism implemented over Hadoop.

This and other tests show there is no one-size-fit-all mechanism for SQL on Hadoop and that early generic solutions, e.g. Hive on MapReduce are not sufficient for more complex scenarios. It is worth mentioning that not only the SQL engine but also the data storage impacts the performance. For example the application of columnar formats, such as Parquet or ORC (Optimized Row

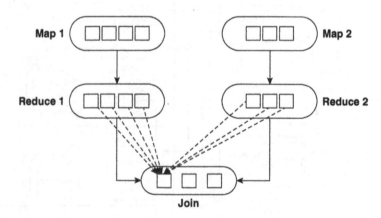

Figure 7.2   Tez data processing.

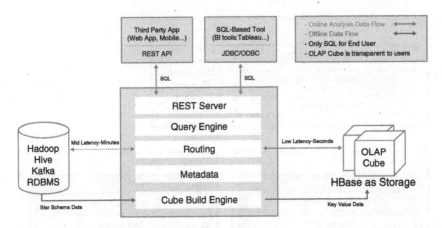

Figure 7.3   High-level architecture of Kylin.

Columnar), can greatly increase the performance of many analytical queries. Abadi et al. [2009].

Kylin is a distributed analytics engine developed at eBay [2014] and later open sourced to become the mainstream Apache project. Apache [b]. It provides an SQL interface and multi-dimensional analysis (OLAP) on Hadoop to allow analytics over extremely large data sets.

The high-level architecture of Kylin is presented in Figure 7.3. It follows some well known techniques, like storing pre-calculated results for all dimension combinations. However, Kylin implements these techniques in the distributed environment of Hadoop, allowing for parallel calculations and merging of the results. This allows representing cube data as key-value data, which can be queried much faster.

Kylin can be easily integrated with dashboards, e.g. Tableu, to provide low-latency interface to business analysts.

An example of a commercial tool for scalable SQL analytics on Hadoop is Atscale. The dedicated tool allows data analysts to design virtual OLAP cubes. The data defined in this way is accessible from several popular business intelligence environments. A machine learning based optimizer helps optimization of complex queries in the background.

7.1.2   From Shark to SparkSQL

Shark was designed as an environment in which both SQL and more complex analytical tasks can be performed efficiently, Xin et al. [2013], which was built on Hive code base. The query is parsed, passed, and transformed into a logical plan. This is further optimized with the use of a cost-based optimizer and a

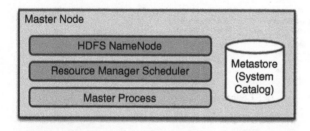

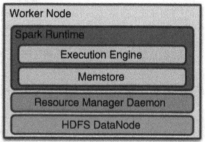

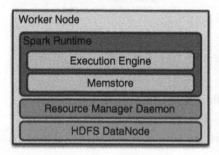

Figure 7.4   Shark architecture.

physical plan of RDD operations for Spark is created. Figure 7.4 shows the overall system architecture.

Most recently Shark has been subsumed by Spark SQL, Armbrust et al. [2015], which is one of the components of the Spark framework for big data processing presented in Section 6.4.1. By embedding the declarative SQL functionality within the entire Spark stack, it is possible to combine it seamlessly with the procedural code needed for more complex processing of unstructured data, machine learning or graph algorithms. The placement of SparkSQL within the data flows is depicted in Figure 7.5.

The basic abstraction in Spark SQL is a DataFrame, a collection of rows, which can be distributed and has a schema. DataFrames have a lot in common with relational tables and, therefore, can be manipulated in the similar way, e.g. filtering or grouping operations. They can be constructed out of existing RDDs or from external data sources.

An important feature of Spark SQL is in-memory caching, which is materialization of data in RAM using columnar storage. This allows for both efficient access as well as for smaller size due to compression.

A lazy approach to execution, which means delaying real processing of data, allows for advanced optimization. A dedicated optimizer, Catalyst, was built to serve this purpose. It supports both rule and cost based optimization and allows extensions to be added by developers.

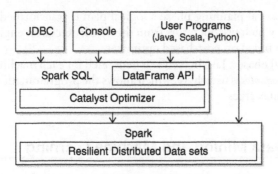

Figure 7.5 Spark SQL data flows.

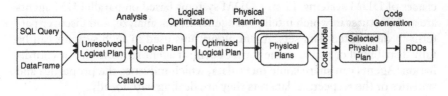

Figure 7.6 Spark SQL query planning

The Catalyst optimizer uses trees as the main data structure. Trees can be manipulated by *rules*, which are functions producing other trees. The pattern matching feature of Scala is used to extract values from the trees. Rules are grouped into batches, which are executed until the tree cannot be changed anymore.

Figure 7.6 shows the phases of Spark SQL query planning. The first phase is analysis of the relations resulting from SQL Parser or a DataFrame. An *unresolved logical plan* tree is built with unbound attributes and data types. Then rules are applied, which:

- look up relations by name from the catalog
- map named attributes to the input provided given operator's children
- determine which attributes refer to the same value to give them a unique ID
- propagate and coerce types through expression

Next comes the logical optimization phase, which applies standard rule-based optimization to the logical plan.

In the physical planning phase a logical plan is transformed into a set of physical ones, which use operators from the Spark execution engine. The final plan is chosen based on cost-based optimizer.

In the final phase a Java bytecode is generated for each machine. The Scala feature of *quasiquotes* is used here, which allows the programmatic construction of abstract syntax trees.

7.2   Big Data Mining and Machine Learning

Distributed Data Mining (DDM) was introduce to speed up the data mining process to handle big data sets and to be able to work in environments with inherent data distribution. Liu et al. [2011] distinguish three different classes of DDM systems. Firstly, DDM systems based on parallel DM agents are architectures in which intelligent agents access, analyze, and discover patterns in distributed data sets. Agent algorithms used in such systems can be fully distributed or utilize some form of central agent responsible for coordination. Agents can share some meta-data, which indicates the properties and statistics of the respective data sets they are dealing with locally.

Another approach to DDM are systems based on meta-learning. Meta-learning in general is the ML sub-domain dealing with "learning to learn." In other words it aims at improving the learning process itself. In the context of DDM, meta-classifiers are created independently based on distributed data sets and a meta-learning algorithm tries to integrate them for best end results.

DDM systems based on Grid are the third option. In this case we try to take advantage of ML algorithm's scalablity and share the load over a large grid of computational resources. Grid computing brings in sever benefits like abstracting the underlying hardware or providing efficient mechanisms for data transfer between the nodes.

Performing data mining on a big data scale is a very challenging task. In real life industry environments, generating valuable insight from the data requires much more that advanced data mining algorithms. Researchers from Twitter highlight two challenges that are often underestimated in theoretical papers on data mining. Lin and Ryaboy [2013]. Firstly, that it is not enough just to have schemas to understand value hidden in data. Secondly, overcoming data heterogeneity requires a huge amount of effort.

The paper also describes the big data mining lifecycle. The cycle consist of the following steps:

- finding the data – most often distributed due to service architecture of the systems

- exploratory data anlalysis – important to assess data quality and plan next steps
- data mining – problem and metrics definition, data preparation, actual mining
- productization of the solution – creating the final robust solution

Further on in Lin and Ryaboy [2013] and in the previous work, Lin and Kolcz [2012], the architecture of the Twitter big data analytics platform is presented. One of the main assumptions for the architecture was to allow easy integration of machine learning algorithms into the whole big data cycle as described above. To this end Pig is used as a tool for managing data flows and machine learning steps are treated just as any other steps of the process.

The framework utilizes stochastic gradient descent for fast one-pass learning and scale out by data partitioning with ensembles. The learners act as data sinks consuming the learning examples but materializing learned models after the learning is finished. Figure 7.7 shows a single classifier (on the left), and a two-classifier ensemble (on the right).

Once the models are learned they have to be deployed on the production. Wrappers have been developed to use classifiers as any other UDF in Pig. A separate UDF handles ensembles. It is also straightforward to measure performance of classifiers and calculate metrics such as precision, recall, area under the curve, etc.

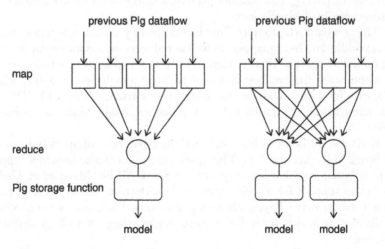

Figure 7.7   Twitter ML architecture – integration of learners into Pig storage functions.

Importantly, the architecture can also scale easily down to a single laptop for easy prototyping of new scripts and algorithms. Minimal modifications are needed to deploy a locally tested solution onto a cluster.

Another example of implementing big data mining architecture is NIMBLE, designed to enable the rapid implementation of parallel ML-DM algorithms on top of Hadoop/MapReduce. Ghoting et al. [2011]. It allows parallel ML-DM algorithms from reusable blocks to be composed.

In the top layer API is provided, which allows implementation of tasks and their respective relation as a DAG. Each task can can take one or more data sets as input, may process the input in parallel, and produce one or more data sets as output. A number of abstract task types are provided, which implement various control/data flows.

The architecture independent layer hosts DAG queue and worker threads to process it. It performs the scheduling and acts as a middleware between the user tasks and architecture dependent layer.

The architecture dependent layer purpose is to allow execution in various computation models on different runtime environments. At the time of writing of the referred paper only MapReduce was implemented.

The NIMBLE architecture and task properties strongly support parallelism. Tasks can spawn other tasks and wait for their completion. They can pass the data as input to support data parallelism. Tasks can be chained into DAGs, which provides possibility for further optimization of the execution. For example, tasks can be co-scheduled inside a single MapReduce job.

A different approach to utilizing Hadoop/MapReduce for DDM is shown in Wu et al. [2011]. The authors present a cloud based DDM architecture utilizing pipelined MapReduce.

The standard MapReduce flow is modified by adding a pipeline, which stores middle data from mappers as well as reducers, so it is immediately available for the next steps. This can significantly speed up the computations under the assumption that reduce function is incrementally computable, which is the case for a large class of algorithms, e.g. sorting, Apriori, TF-IDF, etc. The comparison of traditional and pipelined MapReduce is visible in Figure 7.8.

Earlier in the book we have analyzed the capabilities of Spark (Chapter 6) and Spark SQL (Section 7.1). The Spark environment also provides support for distributed machine learning with its Spark MLlib. Meng et al. [2016]. It provides support for a wide range of algorithms including decision trees, linear models, naive Bayes, clustering methods, PCA, and several others. MLlib also provides tools for feature engineering, as well as statistical packages.

An important feature of MLlib is the Pipeline API, which allows easy creation of ML pipelines out of individual components, transformations,

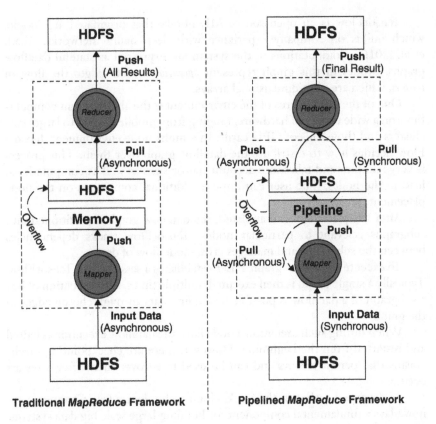

Figure 7.8   Pipelined MapReduce.

and algorithms. There are two types of steps, *transformers* and *estimators*. A transformer is an operation which takes one DataFrame and produces another. They are used for feature operations. Learned models are also transformers. In the latter case, the output is a DataFrame with classes (classifier model) or predictions or any other output that the model generates.

The other type of step in a pipeline is an *Estimator*, which represents the learning algorithm. In this case the input is the learning data and the output is the model, which we know from the above is a transformer. Pipelines, as well as individual models, can be persisted for future use.

A lot of efficiency gains come from tight integration with Spark core libraries, which are well suited for iterative computations needed in many ML algorithms. Also other Spark components empower ML projects. Spark SQL makes data manipulation and pre-processing easy, while together with Spark streaming, online learning on streaming data is possible.

TensorFlow is an open-source ML library that originated at Google, which builds on company experience with deep neural networks. Abadi et al. [2016]. Computations in the system are expressed as stateful dataflow graphs. Nodes in this graph represent *operations*, while edges the flow of *tensors*, which are multidimensional arrays.

One of the key features of the environment is the ability to run computations on a wide variety of hardware, ranging from mobile devices to large scale clusters and thousands of GPU cards. In a multi-node environment Tensor-Flow decides how to distribute the dataflow graph over them. This process is very complex and takes into account tensor sizes as well as computational load in the nodes. The user can impose additional constraints on the node placement.

After the placement is completed, the dataflow graph is partitioned into subgraphs relevant to particular nodes. TensorFlow tracks dependencies between the subgraphs and manages cross-node flow of data.

To execute a dataflow graph a user establishes a session with TensorFlow. Typically a single graph is then executed multiple times. Also execution of just a subgraph of a dataflow is possible by feeding data through chosen edges of the graph.

When during such execution a node fails, the dataflow execution is halted and restarted from the beginning. However, there are checkpointing mechanisms that persist tensors and can be used to recover them after a restart occurs.

As discussed earlier in the book, cloud technologies (see Chapter 5) are nowadays a fundamental component for building large scale big data systems. The same applies for doing large scale ML computations and vendors of cloud services, cloud management platform, and other related services started to reflect this in their architectures and offerings.

Kubeflow is an open source machine learning toolkit for Kubernetes. Its purpose is to streamline deployment and management of ML workflows. It allows the use of Jupyter notebooks on JupyterHub as well as building and deploying Tensorflow models. The power of cloud computing comes here with great scalability possibilities, so that additional CPUs or GPUs resources can be added seamlessly.

Building machine learning models is fundamental to extracting useful knowledge from big data. However, scaling known ML algorithms to operate on extremely large, distributed data sets is not an easy task. Also, ML practitioners are used to specific tools and languages and they expect to work in a similar way with new architectures.

MLbase, Kraska et al. [2013], is an attempt to provide high level abstractions for ML with the power of big data parallel processing underneath.

The system consists of a master and a number of slave nodes. Users interact with the master and specify requests in a declarative MLbase language. Then a Logical Learning Plan (LLP) is built to describe the ML workflow to be executed. A dedicated optimizer has been developed to perform the task of LLP construction.

The next step in the process is a Physical Learning Plan (PLP), which is a set of executable ML operations. These operations are distributed among the slave nodes. The results are returned and joined at the master node and presented to the user.

An important feature, which is taken into account is quality assessment of the models. This factor is also analyzed during the plan optimization phase, since various plans can yield different quality models.

Another feature of the architecture is that it can work continuously on finding better and better models, while providing the best model at a given time to the user. This is very convenient for interactive work as well as for the dynamic big data environment.

Last but not least it is worth mentioning, that the framework is open for extension by new ML algorithms. Each such addition is described by a strict contract, which includes algorithm type, parameters, computational complexity, optimization possibilities (e.g. synchronous versus asynchronous learning).

7.2.1 Graph Mining

Graphs are an elegant formalism suitable for representing several abstract notions as well as natural phenomena, e.g. citation graphs, social networks, World Wide Web to name a few. Typically the algorithms such as PageRank, connected components, diameter estimation, etc. are computed in order to provide insight into the graph properties. Moreover, the size of graphs for real life problems we want to analyze has grown to the point where single machine algorithms are not trackable. Therefore, most recent effort has been devoted to finding architectures and algorithms for distributed processing of very large graphs.

Mining of big data sets represented as graphs requires specific approaches, tools, and architectures. The big graph mining architectures can be broken down into two groups. One build on top of MapReduce, e.g. Pegasus, Kang and Faloutsos [2013], and others, which use other computational models, e.g. Mahout.

Pegasus is an open source graph mining software built on top of MapReduce. It uses Generalized Iterative Matrix-Vector (GIM-V) multiplication as a primitive, which unifies several graph mining algorithms by formulating them as iterative message exchanges with adjacent nodes. It can be observed that the message exchange is equivalent to performing matrix vector multiplication on the adjacency matrix of the graph and the vector containing current states of nodes.

In Kang and Faloutsos [2013] an efficient MapReduce implementation of GIM-V algorithm is provided. In its basic version in the first stage, the matrix elements and the vector elements are joined to make partial results, where the column id of the matrix elements and the row id (index) of the vector elements are used as keys. In the second stage, the partial results are aggregated to make an output vector (Algorithm 4).

Algorithm 1: GIM-V algorithm

---

begin
    for $j \in 1..n$ **do**
        $x_j \leftarrow combine2(M_{i,j}, v_j)$
    $combineAll(x_1, \ldots, x_n)$
    $assign(v_i, v_{new})$

---

where M is an n by n matrix, v is a vector of length n.

Several improvements to this basic setup have been proposed. For example, it is possible to cluster the non-zero elements of the adjacency matrix, encode it using blocks, and compress it to decrease the amount of data traffic in MapReduce computation.

7.2.2 Agent Based Machine Learning and Data Mining

Agent mining is an interdisciplinary field, which combines efforts of multi-agent systems, data mining, machine learning, and other related fields. The motivation to join these fields is to take advantage of known ML/DM algorithms on the one hand, while utilizing flexibility and efficiency in distributed computation provided by multi-agent systems. Cao et al. [2009].

Zhang et al. [2005] list the following advantages of using agents for DDM tasks:

- retaining the autonomy of the data sources
- facilitating interactive distributed data mining
- improving dynamic selection of sources and data gathering
- having high scalability to massive distributed data
- stimulating multi-strategy distributed data mining
- enabling collaborative data mining

In Liu et al. [2011] the authors propose a novel DDM model called DRH-PDM (Data source Relevance-based Hierarchical Parallel Distributed data mining Model).

The model utilizes Web Service technology for seamless integration of components. Depending on the data relevance the sources are aggregated into Local Centralized Data Mining Layer (LCDML) or Local Parallel Data Mining Layer (LPDML). A Global Processing Unit (GPU) integrates the results.

The DRHPDM mining workflow consists of the following steps:

- Submission of DM requirements to the GPU by the user
- The DM request is divided into a number of DM sub-tasks
- Distribution of subtasks to the sites
- The site receives tasks and registers data sets at GPU
- Data set information is combined and grouped logically
- Sites are notified to start DM processes
- The DM results (models) are transferred to Local Managing Agent (LMA) for local integration
- The final global model is transformed and submitted to the user

Another example of agent application in DDM is presented in Chaimontree et al. [2012], where a Multi-Agent Based Clustering (MABC) framework is described. The clustering process consists of two parts. Firstly, based on the specific clustering algorithms, the initial clustering configuration is generated. In the second phase agents negotiate with each other to improve the initial configuration.

Four types of agent are distinguished in MABC:

- user agents
- data agents
- validation agents
- clustering agents

User agents provide the interface to the system. They receive the request, spawn clustering agents and return the result. Data agents manage the available data sources. There is one data agent dedicated for each source. Clustering agents run the main clustering algorithms. Finally, validation agents validate and return results.

There is one clustering agent for each cluster. They have the ability to merge and spawn as the number of clusters changes. Depending on the algorithm, clustering agents "bid" on the records, which do not belong to any of the clusters yet.

An architecture for data mining in the cloud environment with the use of multi-agent systems is presented in Othmane and Hebri [2012]. Each user task is represented by a single task agent. The task agent is creating other instances of agents needed to complete the task such as: data agents, mining agents, and visualization agents.

Data agents are responsible for accessing, extracting, and preprocessing of the necessary data. Such prepared data sets are stored in the temporary cloud storage. The mining agents implement the specific DM algorithm, which will be used to process the data. To achieve optimal efficiency mining agents create process agents, which are performing the individual computation tasks that can be done in parallel. The visualization agents present the results in the user interface.

CHAPTER 8

Physically Distributed Systems – Mobile Cloud, Internet of Things, Edge Computing

I n Chapter 5 we have analyzed architectures for performing large scale computations in the cloud, primarily in the Infrastructure as a Service (IaaS) model. This works well for systems that can be broken down into a number of services and accessed by light-weight, typically web-based, clients. However, things get more complicated when parts of our system are physically distributed devices, which can be equipped in unique sensors and actuators, but have limited computational capabilities. In the age of big data we want to take advantage of the data generated and stored across our infrastructure and be able to take informed decisions at any physical point of our networked resources.

In other words, this chapter takes a closer look at how modern big data architectures distribute computing in order to optimize efficiency, latency, and other KPIs. On the one hand, we look deeper into the cloud technologies, allowing for offloading and scaling of large computations. On the other hand, modern ubiquitous environments and the growing power of distributed devices enables computation to move towards the network edge, which minimizes the need for data transfers as well as reduces the latency. By utilizing both we can build powerful solutions for big data applications.

The first example of such setups are *mobile cloud* systems, which enable users of mobile devices (typically smart phones) to use rich applications and services, supported by the computational resources available in the cloud. Secondly, we look at edge computing, another innovative idea, which moves critical computations towards end user devices and physical sensors in order to optimize their performance and control. Later on in the chapter, we will look at the Internet of Things (IoT), which is a fast growing paradigm for connecting devices and designing protocols for their autonomous collaboration. Finally, more "futuristic" ideas such as fog computing will be described.

The boundaries between the above concepts are not clean cut, as they often try to solve the similar problem. For example, the idea of a *cloudlet* can be regarded at the same time as the evolution of mobile cloud as well as the beginning of edge computing. Similarly, ad-hoc cooperative clouds are very similar to the fog computing paradigm. As a result, while the next sections make a clear division between the concepts to provide more focus, the reader will see that the particular challenges and solution will reappear and blend with each other. As there is never a "one-size-fits-all" solution to complex problems, the ultimate goal of this chapter is to compare different approaches with all their advantages and limitations.

With the proliferation of smart devices and systems based on them, initiatives for standardization of the complex landscape started to emerge. For example ETSI, a European Standards Organization focused on telecommunication, broadcasting and networks in general, has been involved with *oneM2M*, a technical specification for M2M (machine to machine) connectivity. The main purpose of oneM2M is to establish a common service layer, which can enable abstraction from heterogeneous hardware and software platform underneath. Swetina et al. [2014]. Such efforts are much needed as the explosion of device types and vendors has led to high diversity of protocols, data formats, control, and monitoring mechanisms, etc.

8.1   Mobile Cloud

According to Khan [2014], *Mobile Cloud Computing (MCC) is an integration of cloud computing technology with mobile devices to make the mobile devices resource-full in terms of computational power, memory, storage, energy, and context awareness.* By doing so, it is possible to provide the users with rich, data intensive applications, available on their mobile devices. Dinh et al. [2013] enumerate the following advantages of mobile cloud computing:

- Extending battery lifetime – significant gains can be achieved by computation offloading to the powerful resources in the cloud.
- Improving data storage capacity and processing power – extending the available capacity by external cloud storage, e.g. multimedia sharing

services, which allow uploading to the cloud of pictures/movies after their creation and do not have to be downloaded back for sharing.

- Improving reliability – taking advantage of native replication available in the cloud improves reliability of mobile services. Also privacy and security issues can be governed in the cloud more easily.

- Other advantages available with the use of cloud: dynamic provisioning, scalability, multitenancy, ease of integration (see Chapter 5 for more details).

All those advantages do not come for free. Whenever a load is pushed to the cloud we have to find the balance between the latency resulting from limited mobile processing capability versus the communication latency to send requests and receive results. Similarly on the energy optimization side processing energy has to be measured against the energy for communication, which can vary substantially depending on the current location. There are no general rules to solve these dilemmas as tasks can also vary significantly, for example with respect to results being available in real time versus the situation when off-line computations can be performed. Finally, security issues should be taken into account. There are threats related to storing sensitive information locally on a personal device and different threats related to other issues such as network transmission, attacks on central databases, identity theft, etc.

Over the years, mobile cloud computing has undergone significant evolution. Gao et al. [2013] distinguish three generations of mobile cloud computing architectures. In the first wave mobile users were able to download mobile apps from application store and utilize personal cloud, often operated by the device or OS vendor, for storage. An example of such early applications are personal multimedia, which allow users to store and and share photographs and movies taken on their mobile devices.

In the second generation personal clouds started to play a lesser role, giving way to enterprise public cloud and large number of mobile SaaS services, optimized towards QoS and user experience. Most of the daily used mobile applications for communication, navigation, entertainment, etc. work in this model.

Finally, third generation of mobile cloud computing brings in more advanced features, including network virtualization solutions and differentiation of cloud architecture into computing cloud and mobile cloud layers. Computing cloud is responsible for back-end mobile application servers while mobile cloud takes care of essential mobile services such as identity management, location aware services, etc. This enabled introduction of highly scalable mobile platforms for millions of users such as multimedia streaming, real time gaming, and many others.

Mobile cloud computing has been subject to standardization efforts. In 2015 the Object Management Group (OMG), an international technology standards consortium, published a Cloud Customer Architecture for Mobile. OMG [2015]. The document points out several motivations for using cloud with mobile computing. It emphasizes the rise of data intensive applications, global distribution of users, short life-cycle of mobile apps driven by frequent hardware updates, diversity of mobile platforms, etc.

In the OMG reference architecture for mobile cloud computing four tiers are distinguished:

- Mobile device – owned by the end user
- Public network – enabling connectivity with the cloud
- Provider cloud environment – hosting cloud services
- Enterprise network – where enterprise assets are located

The mobile device holds the mobile applications with which the user interacts. In a corporate setup there is additionally a *management agent* that can be placed on the device in order to enforce enterprise policies and security rules.

Public network components, apart from telecommunication infrastructure, include services, which enable connectivity of the mobile device with the cloud. These services typically include DNS, firewall, load balancing, and Content Delivery Networks (CDN).

Provider cloud holds a number of services needed for providing needed cloud services, which include:

- Mobile gateway – acts as the entry point for mobile devices to the back-end services by exposing relevant APIs and ensuring security
- Mobile backend – hosts backend logic and data accessible via the mobile gateway
- Mobile device management – used in the enterprise setup allows tracking and management of mobile devices by keeping centralized registries and synchronizing with the distributed management agents installed on the devices
- Mobile business applications – provide advanced functionalities such as analytics, workflow management, etc.
- API management – enable efficient navigation and discovery in the complex API landscape
- Data services – implement storage of data and access to relevant data assets in the cloud services and in the enterprise in-house systems

- Security services – ensure only authorized users have access to specific services and data
- Enterprise transformation and connectivity – needed in the cases of more complex data transformations between the services and the applications

Finally, the enterprise network components hold the user directory, sensitive data assets, and enterprise in-house services.

The general architecture for mobile cloud computing is depicted in Figure 8.1. According to this view, mobile network providers take care of the connectivity of mobile devices to the Internet. This allows access to the cloud services and resources. Typically four groups of cloud resources for mobile cloud computing are distinguished:

- Distant immobile clouds – large public cloud providers (e.g. Amazon AWS, Microsoft Azure, etc.)
- Proximate immobile computing entities – local data centers, often governed by the mobile network providers
- Proximate mobile computing entities – various mobile devices, i.e. smart phones, tablets, other hand helds, and wearable devices
- Hybrid – combination of the above

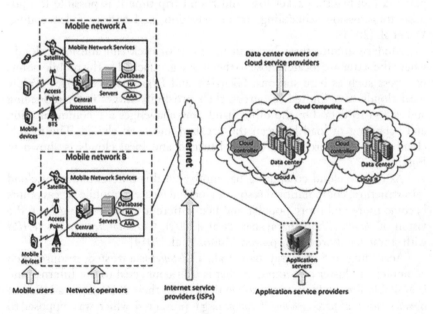

Figure 8.1   Mobile cloud computing architecture.

A mobile cloud computing environment needs to work under the constraints of available network resources, i.e. WiFi or mobile internet. Traditionally, mobile cloud computing providers had to deal with a difficult optimization task of computation offloading under varying bandwidth. For example Misra et al. [2013] propose an auction-based QoS-guaranteed utility maximization algorithm, where mobile nodes purchase bandwidth from the service provider. Continuous progress in mobile technologies, e.g. introduction of 5G networks, give the promise of relaxing those constraints. However, data intensive (especially multimedia-reach like gaming) application can saturate any available capacity.

Real-time mobile games, especially in the multiplayer mode, were one of the earliest adopters of the mobile cloud computing model. Rendering of complex visualizations in real time is very computational heavy and computational limitations of mobile devices impose a challenge on porting of games available on powerful desktops and consoles. On the other hand the number of mobile device users interested in entertainment is huge.

One approach to mobile video games is performing all rendering on the cloud side and reduce the mobile device to display HFR (High Frame Rate) video. Several algorithms have been proposed to introduce adaptive algorithms that would take network limitations into account and provide streaming with minimal delay and distortion. By constantly monitoring network bandwidth, packet loss, and round trip time it is possible to optimize transmission scheduling, frame selection, and custom video coding. Wu et al. [2015].

Modern architectures bring in the ideas of back-end and local clouds, where the latter are located close to the user, e.g. attached to the mobile points of access such as base stations. Gkatzikis and Koutsopoulos [2013]. While local clouds have limited resources, their proximity allows faster offloading and access to data. On the other hand new challenges are communication and balancing of load between the backend and local clouds. The mobile cloud computing architecture with backend and local clouds is shown in Figure 8.2.

As mobile cloud computing has motivated this differentiation of cloud infrastructure, computational resources located closer to mobile access points become more and more popular and take different forms, starting from the vision of *cloudlets*, Satyanarayanan et al. [2009], to *femto-access points (FAPs)* with storage and processor power. Munoz et al. [2014].

According to Satyanarayanan et al., a *Cloudlet* is a trusted, resource-rich computer or cluster of computers that is well-connected to the Internet and is available for use by nearby mobile devices. In their 2009 paper a vision of *cloudlet-based resource-rich mobile computing* is presented, which was supposed to

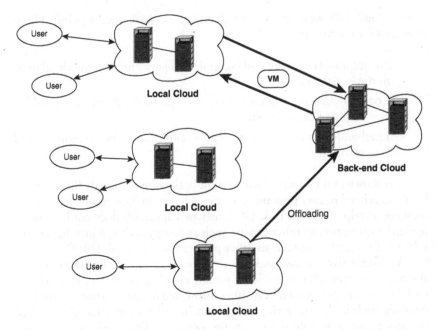

Figure 8.2   Mobile cloud computing architecture with backend and local clouds.

lead to proliferation of self-managing *data centers in a box*. According to this vision, such local computational resources would be widely used even by local non-IT business for the benefit of their customers. While we know today that this has not became a reality, those ideas definitely acted as inspiration for the next generation of cloud architectures for mobile, big data applications.

The concept of a *femtocell* is a home base-station installed locally to improve voice and data coverage in mobile networks. Chandrasekhar et al. [2008]. This idea has been further extended into *femto-cloud*, which is a set of femto-access points (FAP). In this setup, an optimization algorithm needs to decide which parts of computation to offload onto the nearby FEP. Munoz et al. [2014].

While mobile cloud computing faces the same challenges as classical cloud computing, with regards to optimizing performance by migrating computations (see Chapter 5 for details), it also brings new dimensions to the equation such as mobility. As the users move and change their point of access, related computations should keep the proximity, so that the latencies can stay at acceptable levels. In Gkatzikis and Koutsopoulos [2013] a scenario is considered in which a user initiated computational task initiates offload to the cloud, followed up by user changing network access point. Three strategies are compared:

- No-migration strategy – all computation performed on the cloud local to the initial location
- Load-only-aware migration strategy – performs migration based on availability of cloud resources
- Load-and-mobility-aware strategy – optimizes for both resources and user proximity

It is shown that by taking into account both computational efficiency and latencies related to user proximity, we can achieve the best results in terms of total round trip of a given task. Obviously this approach does not have to be optimal with respect to other criteria such as energy saving, which has been a subject of research in numerous other publication. Gai et al. [2016].

An alternative to the backend or proximate clouds described in the above architectures, it is possible for mobile cloud computing to form ad-hoc mobile clouds, also called *cooperation-based architectures*, which consist of multiple mobile devices acting as a cloud in order to provide cloud based services to other mobile devices in the network. The motivation for such an approach is that powerful centralized cloud services may not always be available, while widespread of co-located mobile devices gives opportunity to share some computational tasks among themselves. In such a setup calls to the backend cloud need to be intercepted and redirected to the nodes in the ad-hoc network.

Huerta-Canepa and Lee propose an architecture which implements the above scenario. Huerta-Canepa and Lee [2010]. In this approach the *Application Manager* modifies the application at launch time and adds a proxy for proper redirection of remote calls. The *resource manager* checks the available resources and matches them with a particular application profile. The next component is the *context manager*, which synchronizes the context between the processes. The *P2P component* keeps track of the devices available in the vicinity. Finally, the *offloading manager* takes care of sending and receiving jobs between the nodes.

Khan [2014] provides a comprehensive survey of application models for mobile cloud computing in which they distinguish the following classes:

- Performance based
- Energy based
- Constraint based
- Multi-objective

Performance based application models focus on offloading computations to the resource rich cloud. An example of such approach is CloneCloud, Chun et al. [2010], which moves computation of parts of the application to the nearby cloud resource. The advantage of this technique is that it does not require special code preparation. The algorithm takes care of cloning of code and state to the cloud, synchronizing suspension of execution on the mobile device, and manages copying of the final state back to the application.

Application models based on energy optimization put energy consumption above computation speed. μCloud is one such model, March et al. [2011], which uses a graph formalism to represent the structure of application composed of heterogeneous components, which can run either on a mobile device or in the cloud. The goal of the model is to optimize the flow between the components from the resource consumption perspective.

Constraint based application models concentrate on limitations of mobile devices and finding alternative cloud resources to fulfill computational tasks. The cloudlet-based approach, Satyanarayanan et al. [2009], presented earlier in this section, falls into this category.

Finally, multi-objective application models try to take into account several optimization criteria, mainly execution time and energy consumption. Examples of such models in literature are MAUI, Cuervo et al. [2010], or ThinkAir, Kosta et al. [2011].

Mobile agents are a useful concept in mobile cloud computing environments. In Angin and Bhargava [2013] a mobile agent-based dynamic performance optimization framework for mobile-cloud computing is presented. It is proposed to break down the mobile applications into partitions modeled as agents. While several functionalities are strictly tied to the physical device, others that perform abstract computations can be offloaded to the cloud by means of mobile agent migration functionality as described in Chapter 2. There is a dedicated component called the *execution manager*, which identifies available cloud resources as well as creates an execution plan for the application. In this plan some of the application partitions will be offloaded as described above.

8.2 Edge and Fog Computing

In the previous section on mobile clouds, the main focus was on how to offload computations from mobile devices, which have limited capabilities, into the resource-rich cloud. However, the trend of cloud differentiation into proximate and remote layer, described earlier in this chapter, indicated this can be a two-way process. As we optimize not only for processing speed, but also latency and energy consumption, the overall architecture can also benefit from moving some of its elements towards the "network edge." This concept is central to the ideas of edge computing and fog computing.

Edge computing can be defined as a new paradigm in which substantial computing and storage resources – variously referred to as cloudlets, micro data centers, or fog nodes – are placed at the Internet's edge in close proximity to mobile devices or sensors. Satyanarayanan [2017]. Fog computing is a highly virtualized platform that provides compute, storage, and networking services between devices and traditional cloud computing data centers, typically, but not exclusively located at the edge of network. Bonomi et al. [2012].

Following the concepts of edge and fog computing brings several benefits. Firstly, it is possible to improve system responsiveness. Even if a backend cloud needs to be accessed, there are typically tasks which can be performed closer to the user, and therefore provide results with lower latency. In such a case even temporary unavailability of the main cloud resources does not have to stop the service or will limit only partly its functionality. Edge resources also improve the scalability of services, as they take some of the load upon themselves, they can also preprocess and cache data before being pushed into the main back-end cloud. For example a mobile navigation system can distribute the relevant sections of the map to the edge nodes for easy access, while recording the traffic information received back from the devices and sharing it with other local users instantly. The updates to the backend cloud in such a scenario are less crucial and can be performed with a higher latency.

Edge computing directly addresses the shift of the role of end user devices, which become not only data consumers, but also data producers. From multimedia, to social interactions, to fitness sensors readings, all this data needs to be recorded, processed, and redistributed.

Limitations in network speed impacts not only the latency, but also the amount of data, which can be transferred to the cloud. With the data generation growing exponentially (as discussed in Chapter 3 on the sources of data), network bandwidth is not keeping pace, while we expect the services to be more and more data intensive. Edge computing gives the possibility of avoiding heavy data transfers and performing computations locally.

Another important aspect of edge computing is increased context awareness. Context can greatly increase the quality of several services such as recommender systems, digital advertising, entertainment, etc. While there are many elements of the contextual information, most of them are by definition determined by the location of the user and, therefore, the latest measurement is available within or near the network edge.

As edge computing found its way to facilitate mobile computing (discussed in the previous section), this fusion is reflected in the emergence of the new term Mobile Edge Computing (MEC). Mach and Becvar [2017]. To perform the MEC concept in practice, three problems need to be solved. Firstly, an algorithm is needed for deciding when to offload, when to do it partially, and when to perform computations locally. Secondly, as MEC has a distributed topology, efficient allocation of computational resources is needed. Finally, the user movement and switching of access points and bandwidth adds to the overall complexity and needs to be taken into account and managed.

Designing an optimal algorithm for offloading decisions needs to take into account several factors such as the state of mobile device resources, the chances of the application getting access to them within the predictable time frame, predicted MEC resources availability, as well as network bandwidth. Liu et al. [2016]. The algorithm is usually located inside the mobile device. If we want to optimize latency as well as energy consumption, the optimization algorithms become even more complex. Partial offloading can help balance these criteria, however not all applications are suitable to break down into smaller jobs. Also the higher task granularity increases the overall complexity of the problem even more.

Allocation of computing resources to the offloaded tasks is performed within the MEC. While there is some research being done on energy consumption, typically the main optimization criteria is the round trip time of the job, as limited battery power is not a factor as in the case of mobile devices. In the simplest case it manages only one node, so the order of tasks is the only optimization option. In more complex setups several MEC nodes can be at hand. In the case of very heavy computations, the MEC node may decide to offload it even further to the resource-rich backend cloud.

Earlier in this chapter we have already analyzed the importance of mobility-aware algorithms for mobile clouds. In the case of MEC, this problem can become even bigger. Edge resources are strategically located to facilitate locality and change of the access point while an offloaded task is being computed, can significantly modify the the topology of the network connection between the mobile device and the server. This is especially the case when switching between wifi and mobile access points. The two main possibilities to tackle this issue is either establishing the new communication path and accepting potential increase in latency or migration of computation to the more optimal MEC node.

8.2.1 Business Case: Mobile Context Aware Recommender System

As discussed in Chapter 7 on big data analytics and machine learning, one of the most important tasks of big data architectures is training of machine learning models. While contemporary big data techniques provide capabilities for building accurate models from huge data sets gathered in the cloud, these models often require context for their final execution. This problem can be solved only partially with approaches such as Lambda Architecture (see Section 6.4.2), which contain a stream processing component. In such a setup, while the computation is close to real time, it is still necessary to pass the context measurement to a centralized component and wait for the result to be returned. This will be too long for several cases, when we want to provide a responsive experience to the user, adapting to his current actions.

A good example of such application are recommender systems. Twardowski and Ryżko [2015] introduce the "model to data" approach to solve this problem in the case of serving recommendations on mobile devices. In the proposed approach the architecture consists of two parts. Firstly, the *server side* follows the multi-agent Lambda as described earlier in Section 6.4.3. It is additionally equipped with the *edge services* layer, the purpose of which is to enable communication between the backend services and the network edge. The main task of the entire server side is computation of the CARS2 model using SGD.

As a supplement to the server side, the architecture extends into the mobile devices owned by the end users. The device collects the data from the relevant sensors as well as the user feedback. Based on this information as well as the precomputed model received from the server side, the final set of recommendations is calculated for the user.

The architecture described above is a very interesting case for this particular book, as it also involves the use of agents as a paradigm for constructing the system. On the server side, each independent component is modeled as an agent. Also on the mobile side functions such as data synchronization, context, and event gathering, final recommendation calculation, etc. are performed by relevant agents. Most importantly the model is transferred within a mobile special agents according to the mobile agent paradigm as described in Section 2.2.

8.3 Internet of Things

This section describes the concept of the Internet of Things (IoT), which refers to connecting physical objects into one network, and has gained significant attention and is subject to extensive research both in academia and industry. We will analyze different approaches and architecture for the IoT, its connection to the concepts of cloud, big data, and multi-agent systems.

8.3.1 IoT Fundamentals

The term *Internet of Things* was initially coined to describe physical objects identified by Radio-Frequency Identification (RFID) technology.

As the number of objects with sensors, actuators, and computational power increased, the term started to take on a broader meaning. The International Telecommunication Union (ITU) defines the IoT as "a global infrastructure for the Information Society, enabling advanced services by interconnecting (physical and virtual) things based on, existing and evolving, interoperable information and communication technologies." ITU [2012]. The Internet of Things can also be viewed as a paradigm where everyday objects can be equipped with identifying, sensing, networking, and processing capabilities that will allow them to communicate with one another and with other devices and services over the Internet to accomplish some "objective." Whitmore et al. [2015].

The IoT contributes to the idea of a *smart world* in which intelligence is ubiquitous and blended in the surrounding objects. According to this vision, the current applications are just the beginning. As the number of IoT devices reaches critical mass and improvements in communication, distributed computation and analytics advance, a wide range of entirely new services will become available, allowing for truly smart homes, cars, cities, etc. These forthcoming services have the potential to change the way we work and live. Smart supply chains will allow goods to reach us at unprecedented speed, biological and environmental data can be analyzed in real time to support our comfort and health, smart vehicles and road infrastructure can improve safety, etc.

Making the vision described above a reality is a huge endeavor. The projected number of IoT devices is a challenge by itself, as fundamental tasks of addressing space outgrow the current capabilities of the Internet, even with the use of IPv6. It is projected that this number will reach 50 billion devices in 2020. Nordrum [2017]. But the ability to uniquely address IoT devices is merely the beginning of the journey. We need to provide many-to-many communication channels for data exchange, computational power for processing, analytics for providing semantics, develop highly distributed algorithms, etc. An important observation is that we are not working in the "green field," as IoT embraces more and more devices surrounding us, which were not designed initially to work as connected, intelligent components of a larger environment (e.g. thermostats, kitchen appliances, cars, etc.). Adaptation of these devices, standardization, and unification will take a long time to accomplish.

Al-Fuqaha et al. [2015] identify the following elements of the IoT:

- Identification – key element for assuring uniqueness of objects and matching them
- Sensing – gathering data from specialized sensors

- Communication – means of transferring the data with emphasis on low-power, low-latency
- Computation – distributed processing capabilities supported by cloud resources
- Services – services build on top of IoT devices
- Semantics – ability to extract knowledge from data

As of today, we can identify a number of key technologies related to the IoT. As the IoT device level progress in sensor technology provides a plethora of very precise, specialized measurement tools. Also widespread technologies such as GPS, Barcode, RFID, etc., generates important information on the device and environment state. On the communication side, advances in the mobile internet with 5G networks making their way and increasing bandwidth for wireless communication, allow for more and more data to be exchanged. Every year the IoT devices themselves become more and more powerful, which brings more processing capabilities. Standardization leads to lower cost of software developments, as embedded programming does not mean porting of an OS for each new device. Section 8.2, cloud and edge computing, play an important role in supporting IoT (see section below).

There is no single reference architecture for the IoT. However, several proposals can be found in the literature. They differ with respect to complexity and the number of distinguished layers.

In the most simple approach three layers are distinguished. Wu et al. [2010]. The *perception layer* is responsible for interaction with physical devices and connecting them to the overall network, by gathering sensor data and exchanging signals for the actuators. The *network layer* provides connectivity by effectively routing messages between devices and services. This layer is not uniform, as it uses various available communication channels including wireless and the Internet. At the top the *application layer* (also called the *business layer*) is located, the role of which is to provide service and operations based on the data available from the lower layers.

In a more complex approach a *five layer* was proposed, with the following components. At the bottom the *perception layer* is located with the purpose similar as the respective layer in 3-layer approach. The *transport layer (aka network layer)* is also similar to the 3-layer counterpart and provides connectivity between the devices and the rest of the system. What the 5-layer approach brings in is the next layer namely the *processing layer*. This addresses the problem of huge amounts of data received in real time from the IoT devices. By applying advanced data processing, analytics, and utilizing cloud technologies, this data overload can be managed. More details on these aspects of the IoT will be discussed in the subsequent sections of this chapter. Another differentiation brought in by the 5-layer architecture is the split between the *application layer* and the *business layer*. While the former role is to implement dedicated applications for specific users and industries, the latter takes care of the business model for these applications, i.e. their release, access, pricing, etc.

Service Oriented Architecture (SOA) (See Chapter 2) has also been an inspiration for IoT architectures. In accordance with the SOA paradigm, a dedicated *service layer* is distinguished above the *network layer*, the role of which is to provide a set of specialized services of which more complex applications (located in the *application layer*) are composed. Among others it should provide the means for service management, discovery, and composition.

While, in the architecture described above, SOA can be viewed as a form of middleware for the IoT, other forms of IoT middleware have also been proposed. ITU [2012], Al-Fuqaha et al. [2015]. The argument for the introduction of sophisticated middle layer comes from the heterogeneity of the IoT environment, which has already been mentioned in this section. From protocols, through data formats to semantics, all these aspects need to be unified if we want to be able to write new services and applications with low cost.

With increasing maturity of the IoT architectures described above and thanks to standardization and introduction of middleware, sensors and actuators could become easily available as any other utility networks, e.g. water, energy, etc. Applications could be developed and installed on top of such utilities with low cost. This however introduces problems with "system of systems" complexity, especially on the actuator end, which need to be overcome. Also the privacy and security issues arise, as in a complex system, it becomes difficult to track who can access what data and manipulate which actuator. As will be discussed later in this section, multi-agent systems are one of the paradigms which can help solve these issues.

The core IoT technologies described above are not adequate to provide advanced services, due to the limited computational resources and complexity of the distributed environment. This can only be achieved by the use of the cloud resources as well as big data analytics, which will be analyzed in the following sections.

8.3.2   IoT and the Cloud

In Chapter 3, about the sources of data, how much data is generated by the IoT has been described. To get actionable insights from this data and build advanced applications, lots of computational power is needed. This power is not available within the IoT devices, which calls for the need for cloud resources. Similarly to the mobile cloud, discussed earlier in this chapter, also in the case of the IoT the cloud can provide backend support for heavy computational jobs, serving results back to end devices and user UI. However, the scale of the problem in the IoT environment is much bigger. The number of IoT devices has already outgrown mobile devices by an order of magnitude and this difference is predicted to grow even further. Also the level of heterogeneity is much bigger with a multitude of hardware and software solutions and limited standardization.

It is important to observe that the benefits from merging the IoT and cloud domains go both ways. While the IoT can take advantage of almost unlimited cloud resources, cloud-based applications can be greatly enriched by the ability to access data about real time events and context and provide feedback with the actuators distributed in real environments. This gives the promise of much better personalization and relevance of the services to the end user.

The availability of *things* located in the physical environments can be viewed as a new paradigm called *things as a service*.

The generic IoT architectures described in the previous section showed there is a strong need for cloud resources for providing storage and processing power. To address these needs, one can use general purpose solutions provided in IaaS, SaaS, DaaS, and other models, to deploy backend services, while more specialized paradigms such as *Sensing and Actuation as a Service (SAaaS)* emerge. DiStefano et al. [2012] propose an architecture for *CoT (Cloud of Things)* depicted in Figure 8.3. At the lowest *IntraNode* level individual nodes are abstracted. The *InterNode* layer deals with integration of various devices into SAaaS Cloud. *InterCloud* provides integration of services provided in the SAaaS model with other services, e.g. IaaS, DaaS, etc. At the very top SaaS offering is built on top of the TaaS cloud.

While it is possible to integrate the IoT with generic cloud offerings, a number of dedicated solutions and environments have emerged. IoTCloud, Fox et al. [2012], is an open source project aimed at abstracting IoT devices via API and integrating them with backend services. IoTCloud architecture, depicted in Figure 8.4, consists of four components:

- IoTCloud controller – takes care of providing services for sensor registration, discovery, subscription, and control, by maintaining relevant metadata about sensors and creating (via Broker) message routes between clients and sensors.

- Message Broker – routes the messages in the form of blocks or streams, according to the routes established by the controller.

- Sensors – physical nodes or computational devices producing time series data and listening to control commands through a software interface.

- Clients – subscribe to and consume the data streams and execute commands to sensors in order to provide IoT based services.

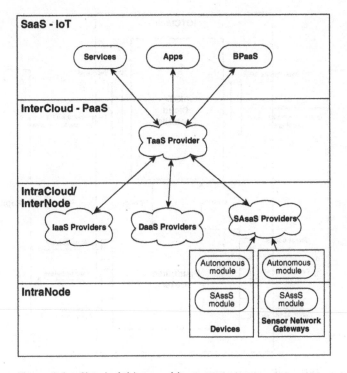

Figure 8.3   Cloud of things architecture.

Suciu et al. [2013] argue that standard cloud infrastructure is not fit for blending with the IoT as it is and propose an architecture for resilient cloud computing and secure IoT. The architecture consists of five major blocks:

- Cloud combination – where management of big data and network resources takes place
- Network management – enabling communication between data centers and virtual nodes
- Sensor IP network – mesh network over IP
- IP network construction – enabling flow of data between the sensors and the cloud
- Sensor control – software control units for the sensors

There are a number of commercial IoTCloud platforms, backed by large vendors, e.g. Microsoft Azure IoT, Google IoT Cloud, AWS IoT, IBM

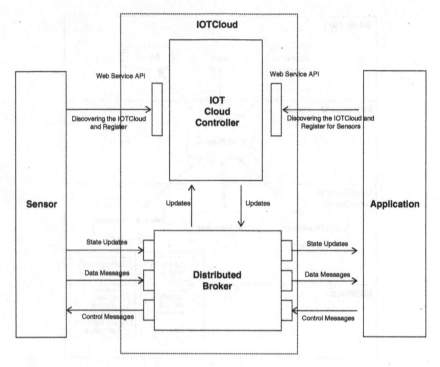

Figure 8.4   IoTCloud architecture.

Watson IoT, SAP IoT, ThingWorx (PTC), etc., as well as a number of smaller vendor solutions, e.g. GENI, Nimbits. FutureGrid Cloud, Open.Sen.se, CloudPlugs, Carriots, COSM, sensor-cloud, and open source solutions, e.g. ThingSpeak. The main advantage of using advanced IoT cloud platforms, is that they bring not only availability of cloud resources, but also several other out-of-the-box features.

One of the main benefits is built-in compatibility with main IoT device vendors. This takes away the burden of understanding and transforming a multitude of protocols and standards.

Another important aspect is tools for implementing logic based on incoming data. This starts from simple rule based systems, to complex event processing capabilities.

Visualization and analytics is yet another important capability of advanced IoT cloud platform. The user should be able, with minimal effort, to create reports, dashboards, graphs, analyze trends, relevant KPIs, and anomalies.

Finally, usually we do not want to keep the collected data in one place, but make it available for other systems through business processes in the company. This brings the need for integration with enterprise platforms, be it procurement, financial, BI, marketing, or any other relevant software. This connectivity is also streamlined by large IoT cloud solutions.

For example Microsoft Azure IoT consists of a number of components providing the above functionalities. The IoT Hub offers secure, bi-directional communication with devices. One can use Azure Functions for simple rule processing and Azure Stream Analytics for complex rule processing. Logics apps allow for integration with business processes. Power BI gives the possibility to create dashboards to monitor the performance of IoT devices in the IoT Central application.

Unsurprisingly, due to the high level of distribution, IoT cloud architectures can build on the concepts of edge computing also discussed earlier in this chapter. Cloud nodes pushed towards the edge of the cloud allow for providing computational power to process data from IoT devices, while offering reasonable latency. The low latency is important for many use cases such as smart grid management or public safety, where the overheads related to the round trip to the backend cloud is not acceptable. To cope with limited bandwidth, MEC servers can perform a number of pre-processing actions such as filtering or aggregation.

Thanks to the use of edge computing, the system lifetime can be extended by saving battery power of the sensors, which offload most computational heavy tasks. On the backend side, congestion to the central systems can be reduced and overall network traffic more optimally distributed.

There are also challenges brought by the introduction of edge computing to the IoT networks. Firstly, with the increased distribution of data storage, enforcing adequate privacy and security becomes a more difficult task. Secondly, resource management in a highly distributed environment is much more complex. Finally, integration of heterogeneous environments is not an easy task.

Ren et al. [2017] build on the *transparent computing* paradigm to introduce an edge-based scalable IoT architecture. The goal of *transparent computing* is to make the details of service provisioning "transparent" to the user, by providing the relevant services in the right place at the right time. Zhang and Zhou [2013]. The programs are stored centrally and streamed and scheduled on demand. The architecture consists of the following components:

- End user layer – composed of IoT devices, which can be viewed as clients
- Edge server layer – all kinds of computational resources located at the network edge
- Core network layer – provides network connectivity between Edge and cloud layers

- Cloud layer – contains powerful resources to support backend of the services
- Management and interface layer – enables control of the entire IoT platform

The publications also provide a case study of wearable IoT devices, which shows the benefits in reduced latency and energy consumption compared to the traditional smart watch.

Given the architectures described in this chapter, that bring in cloud and edge computing to the IoT world, it is possible to have big data computation in IoT systems. One of the main motivators for this is reducing the data volume to the relevant parts. A number of techniques such as PCA, pattern reduction, dimension reduction, feature selection, etc. can be applied.

There is the need for general purpose IoT big data analytics, which can be used for various applications and scenarios. An example of such an approach is TSaaaS (Time Series Analytics as a Service), Xu et al. [2014], implemented as an extension to the time series database service in the IBM cloud platform. It shows significant efficiency gains compared to traditional approaches.

8.3.3   MAS in IoT

Multi-agent systems have, for a long time, been adopted as one of the paradigms for designing and building systems for dynamic sensor networks or more recently for the IoT. The properties of agents, which are intelligent, autonomous, and proactive, naturally fit into the scenarios of distributed environments, where computation and decision-making cannot always be performed in a centralized way.

In the architectures described in the previous sections IoT devices were modeled as end points, which can be called through some strictly defined API calls. Following multi-agent paradigms we can model devices and sensors physically located in the environment as agents. In such a setup the term Cooperative Smart Objects (CSOs) is sometimes used. Multi-agent modeling brings into the IoT world rich patterns and models for autonomous actions on predefined goals as well as distributed algorithms and protocols for cooperative problem solving in a loosely coupled dynamic environment.

Some researchers suggest agents to enable IoT devices to more easily form ad-hoc networks. For example, agent-based clustering methods are proposed to improve power efficiency as well as synchronization for data integrity. López et al. [2011].

Multi-agents and the cloud computing paradigms can come together in order to facilitate IoT solutions. Fortino et al. [2014] propose cloud-assisted and agent-based IoT (CA-IoT) architecture. The agent based component of the system is called Agent-Based Cooperating Smart Objects (ACOSO). In this approach, agent-based middleware allows for cooperation of smart objects modeled as CSOs with each other as well as with non-CSO entities. The main components of a CSO are:

- Task management subsystem – manages the reactive and proactive tasks of CSOs
- Communication Management subsystem – enables communication either as direct asynchronous ACL messaging or publish/subscribe through topics
- Device management subsystem – manages the sensing/actuation devices that belong to the CSO
- Knowledge based management subsystem

The cyber-physical environment of CSOs is supported by a cloud environment, which extends the storage and computational capabilities of the agents.

An important area of mobile agent applications are sensor networks and most recently wireless sensor networks. The number of geographically distributed sensors grow rapidly and it is not possible to equip them with all possible applications for processing, monitoring, and control. With limited bandwidth and power supply (often provided by batteries) it is also not efficient to transmit all of the data from source nodes to the sink.

Mobile agents address these issues, by providing in one model, mobility of the code and data. Mobile code allows particular applications to move to the node where it is optimally located with regard to computational power, power supply, available sensors, data flow, etc. At the same time data dissemination can be performed. An agent collects valuable raw data or results of computations on raw data and moves to the sink node after collection is completed.

Practical applications of mobile agents include visual sensor networks for processing images captured by distributed cameras and tracking targets moving in the physical space. Chen et al. [2007].

In Fok et al. [2009] a mobile agent middleware for self-adaptive wireless sensor networks called Agilla is presented. It allows implementation of applications consisting of a number of agents, which share a wireless sensor network by moving or cloning across the nodes.

To address relations between the agents and physical resources the abstraction of tuple space has been used. A tuple space is a type of shared memory in which data is structured as tuples that are accessed via pattern-matching. The tuple spaces are not shared between the nodes to support greater scalability. Agents can access local and remote tuples.

Furthermore, the platform provides neighbor lists and locations, which are crucial for most WSN applications. Locations are handled explicitly, so an agent can perform an action by referring to a location and not to a particular node. The platform automatically finds a node present at a required location.

Mobile agents can also facilitate the task of offloading computations from low powered devices such as mobile phones into the cloud of more powerful servers. Fernando et al. [2013]. Traditionally the offloading can be achieved by a client-server communication, e.g. by utilizing RPC mechanisms. In a more advanced approach VM migration can be applied. This allows for a more flexible development process with code being written only once. Yet, VM introduces large overhead related to starting and stopping of the VM entities. Mobile agents provide an elegant, efficient, and most flexible solution the the offloading problem. Kristensen [2010].

In mobile cloud environment agents can also be used to support mobility by moving from server to server along with the movements of the user. In the Hydra project, Satoh [2005], such mobility is supported by further controlling the dependence between the components. A special "hook" mechanism is implemented in order to control the migration process of dependent agents.

CHAPTER 9
Summary

I n the course of this book we have taken a journey through contemporary big data architectures. Starting from the evolution of paradigms for building large scale information systems, we have seen how the stage has changed, until big data technologies have been able to become mainstream.

Later in the book we looked at how we obtain extremely large data sets by identifying the most important sources of data. From the Internet, through science to the Internet of Things (IoT), we compared what is specific about each domain and why is it challenging to keep up with its progress.

After understanding where the data came from, we iterated over some of the most relevant tasks, which require computations over big data sets. We analyzed what it takes to generate recommendations and optimize search results, how to derive insights from social media or control smart grid as well as many other tasks.

As cloud computing is nowadays a cornerstone of most large scale computations, we looked at cloud architectures as the foundation for topics described further on. Issues related to cloud management were described as well as distributed storage systems.

Chapter 6 brought the central ideas of the book, starting with basic computational models, then running through stream processing concepts and frameworks and moving to more complex architectures, where both stream and batch processing takes place.

After covering major big data architectures we were able to show how to use them in order to provide analytical capabilities. This ranges from (seemingly) simple topics of providing SQL access in big data environments to large scale machine learning frameworks.

Finally, taking into account the physical distribution of systems such as mobile devices, the IoT, sensor networks, etc., we looked at how to provide big data driven support for concepts such as cyber physical spaces, smart homes and cities, edge and fog computing, etc.

While the book does not aspire to be a comprehensive survey of the big data landscape, the above overview of topics shows that the most important concepts have been covered. Multiple references to the literature provide easy links to gaining deeper insights into the specific areas of interest.

What is specific about the book, and is explicitly stated in the subtitle, is the perspective of the big data domain taken from another field which is multi-agent systems. The relation between the domains is two-fold. Firstly, the book proves a certain thesis, that evolution of mainstream paradigms for building information systems drives the fundamental building blocks towards properties known from the multi-agent domain. Especially in the case of topics covered towards the end of the book, such as IoT or fog computing, it is clearly visible that in many cases it is no longer possible to build robust, scalable systems without distribution of its intelligent components and high degree of their autonomy.

Secondly, intelligent agents find wide applications and provide inspiration for different aspects of big data architectures. Multiple examples of this can be found throughout all chapters. From cloud management, through distributed data mining, to smart factories, agents have been proposed and implemented as a viable solution.

BIBLIOGRAPHY

Daniel J Abadi, Peter A Boncz, and Stavros Harizopoulos. Column-oriented database systems. *Proceedings of the VLDB Endowment*, 2(2):1664–1665, 2009.

Martín Abadi, Ashish Agarwal, Paul Barham, Eugene Brevdo, Zhifeng Chen, Craig Citro, Greg S Corrado, Andy Davis, Jeffrey Dean, Matthieu Devin, et al. Tensorflow: Large-scale machine learning on heterogeneous distributed systems. *arXiv preprint arXiv:1603.04467*, 2016.

Obama Administration. Big data is a big deal, 2012. URL https://obamawhitehouse.archives.gov/blog/2012/03/29/big-data-big-deal.

Ian F Akyildiz and Mehmet Can Vuran. *Wireless sensor networks*, volume 4. John Wiley & Sons, 2010.

Mahmoud Al-Ayyoub, Yaser Jararweh, Mustafa Daraghmeh, and Qutaibah Althebyan. Multi-agent based dynamic resource provisioning and monitoring for cloud computing systems infrastructure. *Cluster Computing*, 18(2): 919–932, 2015.

Ala Al-Fuqaha, Mohsen Guizani, Mehdi Mohammadi, Mohammed Aledhari, and Moussa Ayyash. Internet of things: A survey on enabling technologies, protocols, and applications. *IEEE communications surveys & tutorials*, 17 (4):2347–2376, 2015.

Amazon. Amazon s3. *https://aws.amazon.com/s3/*, a.

Amazon. Amazon autoscaling, b. URL https://docs.aws.amazon.com/autoscaling/ec2/userguide/what-is-amazon-ec2-auto-scaling.html.

Henrique Andrade, Bugra Gedik, K-L Wu, and Philip S Yu. Processing high data rate streams in system s. *Journal of Parallel and Distributed Computing*, 71(2):145–156, 2011.

Javier Andreu-Perez, Carmen CY Poon, Robert D Merrifield, Stephen TC Wong, and Guang-Zhong Yang. Big data for health. *IEEE J Biomed Health Inform*, 19(4):1193–1208, 2015.

Pelin Angin and Bharat K Bhargava. An agent-based optimization framework for mobile-cloud computing. *JoWUA*, 4(2):1–17, 2013.

Apache. Hdfs architecture guide, a. URL http://hadoop.apache.org/docs/stable/hadoop-project-dist/hadoop-hdfs/HdfsDesign.html.

Apache. Apache kylin. http://kylin.apache.org, b. URL http://kylin.apache.org.

Apache. Apache flink - stateful computations over data streams, 2019a. URL https://flink.apache.org/.

Apache. Apache kafka, 2019b. URL https://kafka.apache.org.

Apache. Spark overview, 2019c. URL https://spark.apache.org/docs/latest/.

Apache. Apache storm, 2019d. URL http://storm.apache.org/index.html.

Michael Armbrust, Reynold S Xin, Cheng Lian, Yin Huai, Davies Liu, Joseph K Bradley, Xiangrui Meng, Tomer Kaftan, Michael J Franklin, Ali Ghodsi, et al. Spark sql: Relational data processing in spark. In *Proceedings of the 2015 ACM SIGMOD International Conference on Management of Data*, pages 1383–1394. ACM, 2015.

John Langshaw Austin. *How to do things with words*. Oxford University Press, 1975.

Franz Baader. *The description logic handbook: Theory, implementation and applications*. Cambridge University Press, 2003.

Payam Barnaghi, Wei Wang, Cory Henson, and Kerry Taylor. Semantics for the internet of things: early progress and back to the future. *International Journal on Semantic Web and Information Systems (IJSWIS)*, 8(1):1–21, 2012.

Christian Becker and Christian Bizer. Dbpedia mobile: A location-enabled linked data browser. *Ldow*, 369:2008, 2008.

Fabio Bellifemine, Agostino Poggi, and Giovanni Rimassa. Jade–a fipa-compliant agent framework. In *Proceedings of PAAM*, volume 99, page 33. London, 1999.

Gema Bello-Orgaz, Jason J Jung, and David Camacho. Social big data: Recent achievements and new challenges. *Information Fusion*, 28:45–59, 2016.

James Bennett, Stan Lanning, et al. The netflix prize. In *Proceedings of KDD cup and workshop*, volume 2007, page 35. New York, NY, USA., 2007.

Berkeley. Compute for science. https://boinc.berkeley.edu/. URL https://boinc.berkeley.edu/.

Tim Berners-Lee. Linked data-design issues. 2006.

Kurt Bollacker, Colin Evans, Praveen Paritosh, Tim Sturge, and Jamie Taylor. Freebase: a collaboratively created graph database for structuring human knowledge. In *Proceedings of the 2008 ACM SIGMOD international conference on Management of data*, pages 1247–1250. ACM, 2008.

Flavio Bonomi, Rodolfo Milito, Jiang Zhu, and Sateesh Addepalli. Fog computing and its role in the internet of things. In *Proceedings of the first edition of the MCC workshop on Mobile cloud computing*, pages 13–16. ACM, 2012.

George EP Box, Gwilym M Jenkins, Gregory C Reinsel, and Greta M Ljung. *Time series analysis: forecasting and control*. John Wiley & Sons, 2015.

Michael Boylan-Kolchin, Volker Springel, Simon D. M. White, Adrian Jenkins, and Gerard Lemson. Resolving cosmic structure formation with the millennium-ii simulation. *Monthly Notices of the Royal Astronomical Society*, 398(3):1150–1164, 2009. doi: 10.1111/j.1365-2966.2009.15191.x. URL + http://dx.doi.org/10.1111/j.1365-2966.2009.15191.x.

EA Brewer. Towards robust distributed systems (podc invited talk). In *PODC*, volume 7, 2000.

Justin Brookman, Phoebe Rouge, Aaron Alva, and Christina Yeung. Cross-device tracking: Measurement and disclosures. *Proceedings on Privacy Enhancing Technologies*, 2017(2):133–148, 2017.

Brad Brown, Michael Chui, and James Manyika. Are you ready for the era of 'big data'. *McKinsey Quarterly*, 4(1):24–35, 2011.

Carrie C Buchanan, Eric S Torstenson, William S Bush, and Marylyn D Ritchie. A comparison of cataloged variation between international hapmap consortium and 1000 genomes project data. *Journal of the American Medical Informatics Association*, 19(2):289–294, 2012.

Christopher J Burges, Robert Ragno, and Quoc V Le. Learning to rank with nonsmooth cost functions. In *Advances in neural information processing systems*, pages 193–200, 2007.

Longbing Cao, Vladimir Gorodetsky, and Pericles A Mitkas. Agent mining: The synergy of agents and data mining. *Intelligent Systems, IEEE*, 24(3):64–72, 2009.

Álvaro Carrera and Carlos A Iglesias. A systematic review of argumentation techniques for multi-agent systems research. *Artificial Intelligence Review*, 44 (4):509–535, 2015.

Kate Carruthers. Internet of things and beyond: Cyber-physical systems. *IEEE Internet of Things Newsletter*, 10, 2014.

Ruben Casado. Lambdoop. a framework for easy development of big data applications, 2013. URL http://www.slideshare.net/Datadopter/lambdoop-a-framework-for-easy-development-of-big-data-applications.

CERN. Worldwide large hadron collider grid (wlcg). URL http://wlcg.web.cern.ch.

CERN. Future ict challenges in scientific research - white paper, 2017. URL http://cds.cern.ch/record/2301895/files/Whitepaper_brochure_ONLINE.pdf.

Santhana Chaimontree, Katie Atkinson, and Frans Coenen. A framework for multi-agent based clustering. *Autonomous Agents and Multi-Agent Systems*, 25(3):425–446, 2012.

Soumen Chakrabarti, Martin Van den Berg, and Byron Dom. Focused crawling: a new approach to topic-specific web resource discovery. *Computer Networks*, 31(11):1623–1640, 1999.

Samy Chambi, Daniel Lemire, Owen Kaser, and Robert Godin. Better bitmap performance with roaring bitmaps. *Software: practice and experience*, 46(5):709–719, 2016.

Vikram Chandrasekhar, Jeffrey Andrews, and Alan Gatherer. Femtocell networks: a survey. *arXiv preprint arXiv:0803.0952*, 2008.

Fay Chang, Jeffrey Dean, Sanjay Ghemawat, Wilson C Hsieh, Deborah A Wallach, Mike Burrows, Tushar Chandra, Andrew Fikes, and Robert E Gruber. Bigtable: A distributed storage system for structured data. *ACM Transactions on Computer Systems (TOCS)*, 26(2):4, 2008.

B Chen and AJ Butte. Leveraging big data to transform target selection and drug discovery. *Clinical Pharmacology & Therapeutics*, 99(3):285–297, 2016.

Guoqiang Jerry Chen, Janet L Wiener, Shridhar Iyer, Anshul Jaiswal, Ran Lei, Nikhil Simha, Wei Wang, Kevin Wilfong, Tim Williamson, and Serhat Yilmaz. Realtime data processing at facebook. In *Proceedings of the 2016 International Conference on Management of Data*, pages 1087–1098. ACM, 2016.

Min Chen, Sergio Gonzalez, and Victor Leung. Applications and design issues for mobile agents in wireless sensor networks. *Wireless Communications, IEEE*, 14(6):20–26, 2007.

Avery Ching. Scaling apache giraph to a trillion edges, 2013. URL https://engineering.fb.com/core-data/scaling-apache-giraph-to-a-trillion-edges/.

Byung-Gon Chun, Sunghwan Ihm, Petros Maniatis, and Mayur Naik. Clonecloud: boosting mobile device applications through cloud clone execution. *arXiv preprint arXiv:1009.3088*, 2010.

Christopher Clark, Keir Fraser, Steven Hand, Jacob Gorm Hansen, Eric Jul, Christian Limpach, Ian Pratt, and Andrew Warfield. Live migration of virtual machines. In *Proceedings of the 2nd conference on Symposium on Networked Systems Design & Implementation-Volume 2*, pages 273–286. USENIX Association, 2005.

Philip R Cohen and C Raymond Perrault. Elements of a plan-based theory of speech acts. *Cognitive science*, 3(3):177–212, 1979.

Walter Colitti, Kris Steenhaut, and Niccolò De Caro. Integrating wireless sensor networks with the web. *Extending the Internet to Low power and Lossy Networks (IP+ SN 2011)*, 2011.

ENCODE Project Consortium et al. An integrated encyclopedia of dna elements in the human genome. *Nature*, 489(7414):57, 2012.

Fabricio F Costa. Big data in biomedicine. *Drug discovery today*, 19(4):433–440, 2014.

W Bruce Croft, Donald Metzler, and Trevor Strohman. *Search engines: Information retrieval in practice*, volume 283. Addison-Wesley Reading, 2010.

Eduardo Cuervo, Aruna Balasubramanian, Dae-ki Cho, Alec Wolman, Stefan Saroiu, Ranveer Chandra, and Paramvir Bahl. Maui: making smartphones last longer with code offload. In *Proceedings of the 8th international conference on Mobile systems, applications, and services*, pages 49–62. ACM, 2010.

Gianpaolo Cugola and Alessandro Margara. Processing flows of information: From data stream to complex event processing. *ACM Computing Surveys (CSUR)*, 44(3):15, 2012.

Ward Cunningham. The wycash portfolio management system. *ACM SIGPLAN OOPS Messenger*, 4(2):29–30, 1993.

Dipankar Dasgupta. Immunity-based intrusion detection system: A general framework. In *Proc. of the 22nd NISSC*, volume 1, pages 147–160, 1999.

DB-engines. Nosql db engines, 2019. URL http://db-engines.com/en/article/NoSQL.

Fernando De la Prieta, Sara Rodríguez, Javier Bajo, and Juan Manuel Corchado. A multiagent system for resource distribution into a cloud computing environment. In *International Conference on Practical Applications of Agents and Multi-Agent Systems*, pages 37–48. Springer, 2013.

Jeffrey Dean and Sanjay Ghemawat. Mapreduce: simplified data processing on large clusters. *Communications of the ACM*, 51(1):107–113, 2008.

Giuseppe DeCandia, Deniz Hastorun, Madan Jampani, Gunavardhan Kakulapati, Avinash Lakshman, Alex Pilchin, Swaminathan Sivasubramanian, Peter Vosshall, and Werner Vogels. Dynamo: amazon's highly available key-value store. In *ACM SIGOPS operating systems review*, volume 41, pages 205–220. ACM, 2007.

Hoang T Dinh, Chonho Lee, Dusit Niyato, and Ping Wang. A survey of mobile cloud computing: architecture, applications, and approaches. *Wireless communications and mobile computing*, 13(18):1587–1611, 2013.

Salvatore Distefano, Giovanni Merlino, and Antonio Puliafito. Enabling the cloud of things. In *2012 Sixth International Conference on Innovative Mobile and Internet Services in Ubiquitous Computing*, pages 858–863. IEEE, 2012.

eBay. Announcing kylin: Extreme olap engine for big data, 2014. URL http://www.ebaytechblog.com/2014/10/20/announcing-kylin-extreme-olap-engine-for-big-data/.

Michael Factor, Kalman Meth, Dalit Naor, Ohad Rodeh, and Julian Satran. Object storage: The future building block for storage systems. In *2005 IEEE International Symposium on Mass Storage Systems and Technology*, pages 119–123. IEEE, 2005.

Eric D Feigelson and G Jogesh Babu. Big data in astronomy. *Significance*, 9(4): 22–25, 2012.

Niroshinie Fernando, Seng W Loke, and Wenny Rahayu. Mobile cloud computing: A survey. *Future Generation Computer Systems*, 29(1):84–106, 2013.

Avrilia Floratou, Umar Farooq Minhas, and Fatma Özcan. Sql-on-hadoop: Full circle back to shared-nothing database architectures. *Proceedings of the VLDB Endowment*, 7(12):1295–1306, 2014.

Ioannis Flouris, Nikos Giatrakos, Antonios Deligiannakis, Minos Garofalakis, Michael Kamp, and Michael Mock. Issues in complex event processing:

Status and prospects in the big data era. *Journal of Systems and Software*, 127: 217–236, 2017.

Chien-Liang Fok, Gruia-Catalin Roman, and Chenyang Lu. Agilla: A mobile agent middleware for self-adaptive wireless sensor networks. *ACM Transactions on Autonomous and Adaptive Systems (TAAS)*, 4(3):16, 2009.

Forbes. 6 predictions for the $203 billion big data analytics market, 2017. URL https://www.forbes.com/sites/gilpress/2017/01/20/6-predictions-for-the-203-billion-big-data-analytics-market/.

Giancarlo Fortino, Antonio Guerrieri, Wilma Russo, and Claudio Savaglio. Integration of agent-based and cloud computing for the smart objects-oriented iot. In *Proceedings of the 2014 IEEE 18th international conference on computer supported cooperative work in design (CSCWD)*, pages 493–498. IEEE, 2014.

Ceph Foundation. Ceph storage. *https://ceph.io/ceph-storage/*.

Geoffrey C Fox, Supun Kamburugamuve, and Ryan D Hartman. Architecture and measured characteristics of a cloud based internet of things. In *2012 international conference on Collaboration Technologies and Systems (CTS)*, pages 6–12. IEEE, 2012.

Keke Gai, Meikang Qiu, Hui Zhao, Lixin Tao, and Ziliang Zong. Dynamic energy-aware cloudlet-based mobile cloud computing model for green computing. *Journal of Network and Computer Applications*, 59:46–54, 2016.

Jerry Gao, Volker Gruhn, Jingsha He, George Roussos, Wei-Tek Tsai, et al. Mobile cloud computing research-issues, challenges and needs. In *2013 IEEE Seventh International Symposium on Service-Oriented System Engineering*, pages 442–453. IEEE, 2013.

Gartner. Gartner it glossary. URL https://www.gartner.com/it-glossary/cloud-management-platforms.

Maíra Gatti, Paulo Cavalin, Samuel Barbosa Neto, Claudio Pinhanez, Cícero dos Santos, Daniel Gribel, and Ana Paula Appel. Large-scale multi-agent-based modeling and simulation of microblogging-based online social network. In *International Workshop on Multi-Agent Systems and Agent-Based Simulation*, pages 17–33. Springer, 2013.

Einollah Jafarnejad Ghomi, Amir Masoud Rahmani, and Nooruldeen Nasih Qader. Load-balancing algorithms in cloud computing: A survey. *Journal of Network and Computer Applications*, 88:50–71, 2017.

Jayshree Ghorpade, Jitendra Parande, Madhura Kulkarni, and Amit Bawaskar. Gpgpu processing in cuda architecture. *arXiv preprint arXiv:1202.4347*, 2012.

Amol Ghoting, Prabhanjan Kambadur, Edwin Pednault, and Ramakrishnan Kannan. Nimble: a toolkit for the implementation of parallel data mining and machine learning algorithms on mapreduce. In *Proceedings of the*

17th ACM SIGKDD international conference on Knowledge discovery and data mining, pages 334–342. ACM, 2011.

Michelle Girvan and Mark EJ Newman. Community structure in social and biological networks. *Proceedings of the national academy of sciences*, 99(12): 7821–7826, 2002.

Lazaros Gkatzikis and Iordanis Koutsopoulos. Migrate or not? exploiting dynamic task migration in mobile cloud computing systems. *IEEE Wireless Communications*, 20(3):24–32, 2013.

Khim-Yong Goh, Cheng-Suang Heng, and Zhijie Lin. Social media brand community and consumer behavior: Quantifying the relative impact of user-and marketer-generated content. *Information Systems Research*, 24(1): 88–107, 2013.

Scott A Golder and Michael W Macy. Diurnal and seasonal mood vary with work, sleep, and daylength across diverse cultures. *Science*, 333(6051):1878–1881, 2011.

Norman Gray, Tobia Carozzi, and Graham Woan. Managing research data in big science. *arXiv preprint arXiv:1207.3923*, 2012.

William Gropp, Ewing Lusk, Nathan Doss, and Anthony Skjellum. A high-performance, portable implementation of the mpi message passing interface standard. *Parallel computing*, 22(6):789–828, 1996.

Jayavardhana Gubbi, Rajkumar Buyya, Slaven Marusic, and Marimuthu Palaniswami. Internet of things (iot): A vision, architectural elements, and future directions. *Future Generation Computer Systems*, 29(7):1645–1660, 2013.

Songtao Guo, Bin Xiao, Yuanyuan Yang, and Yang Yang. Energy-efficient dynamic offloading and resource scheduling in mobile cloud computing. In *IEEE INFOCOM 2016-The 35th Annual IEEE International Conference on Computer Communications*, pages 1–9. IEEE, 2016.

Andrew C Harvey and Simon Peters. Estimation procedures for structural time series models. *Journal of Forecasting*, 9(2):89–108, 1990.

Ibrahim Abaker Targio Hashem, Ibrar Yaqoob, Nor Badrul Anuar, Salimah Mokhtar, Abdullah Gani, and Samee Ullah Khan. The rise of "big data" on cloud computing: review and open research issues. *Information Systems*, 47: 98–115, 2015.

Michael A Hayes and Miriam AM Capretz. Contextual anomaly detection in big sensor data. In *Big Data (BigData Congress), 2014 IEEE International Congress on*, pages 64–71. IEEE, 2014.

Harry Hemingway, Folkert W Asselbergs, John Danesh, Richard Dobson, Nikolaos Maniadakis, Aldo Maggioni, Ghislaine JM Van Thiel, Maureen Cronin, Gunnar Brobert, Panos Vardas, et al. Big data from electronic health records for early and late translational cardiovascular research: challenges and potential. *European heart journal*, 39(16):1481–1495, 2017.

Jim Hendler. Web 3.0 emerging. *Computer*, 42(1):111–113, 2009.

Herodotos Herodotou, Harold Lim, Gang Luo, Nedyalko Borisov, Liang Dong, Fatma Bilgen Cetin, and Shivnath Babu. Starfish: A self-tuning system for big data analytics. In *CIDR*, volume 11, pages 261–272, 2011.

Carl Hewitt, Peter Bishop, and Richard Steiger. A universal modular actor formalism for artificial intelligence. In *Proceedings of the 3rd international joint conference on Artificial intelligence*, pages 235–245. Morgan Kaufmann Publishers Inc., 1973.

Charles C Holt. Forecasting seasonals and trends by exponentially weighted moving averages. *International journal of forecasting*, 20(1):5–10, 2004.

J Brian Houston, Joshua Hawthorne, Mildred F Perreault, Eun Hae Park, Marlo Goldstein Hode, Michael R Halliwell, Sarah E Turner McGowen, Rachel Davis, Shivani Vaid, Jonathan A McElderry, et al. Social media and disasters: a functional framework for social media use in disaster planning, response, and research. *Disasters*, 39(1):1–22, 2015.

Gonzalo Huerta-Canepa and Dongman Lee. A virtual cloud computing provider for mobile devices. In *proceedings of the 1st ACM workshop on mobile cloud computing & services: social networks and beyond*, page 6. ACM, 2010.

Kai Hwang, Jack Dongarra, and Geoffrey C Fox. *Distributed and cloud computing: from parallel processing to the internet of things*. Morgan Kaufmann, 2013.

Rob J Hyndman and George Athanasopoulos. *Forecasting: principles and practice*. OTexts, 2018.

IBM. The four vs of big data. URL https://www.ibmbigdatahub.com/infographic/four-vs-big-data.

IRIS. Iris dmc data statistics. URL http://ds.iris.edu/data/distribution/.

Michael Isard, Mihai Budiu, Yuan Yu, Andrew Birrell, and Dennis Fetterly. Dryad: distributed data-parallel programs from sequential building blocks. In *ACM SIGOPS Operating Systems Review*, volume 41, pages 59–72. ACM, 2007.

ITU. Overview of the internet of things, 2012. URL https://www.itu.int/ITU-T/recommendations/rec.aspx?rec=y.2060.

Manar Jaradat, Moath Jarrah, Abdelkader Bousselham, Yaser Jararweh, and Mahmoud Al-Ayyoub. The internet of energy: smart sensor networks and big data management for smart grid. *Procedia Computer Science*, 56:592–597, 2015.

Dawei Jiang, Gang Chen, Beng Chin Ooi, Kian-Lee Tan, and Sai Wu. epic: an extensible and scalable system for processing big data. *Proceedings of the VLDB Endowment*, 7(7):541–552, 2014.

Nicolai M Josuttis. *SOA in practice: the art of distributed system design*. O'Reilly Media, Inc., 2007.

U Kang and Christos Faloutsos. Big graph mining: algorithms and discoveries. *ACM SIGKDD Explorations Newsletter*, 14(2):29–36, 2013.

Ilyas Alper Karatepe and Engin Zeydan. Anomaly detection in cellular network data using big data analytics. In *European Wireless 2014; 20th European Wireless Conference; Proceedings of*, pages 1–5. VDE, 2014.

Samee Ullah Khan. A survey of mobile cloud computing application models. *IEEE COMMUNICATIONS SURVEYS & TUTORIALS*, 16(1), 2014.

Ralph Kimball and Margy Ross. *The data warehouse toolkit: the complete guide to dimensional modeling*. John Wiley & Sons, 2011.

Tomasz Kogut, Dominik Ryżko, and Karol Gałązka. Information retrieval from heterogeneous knowledge sources based on multi-agent system. In *Intelligent Tools for Building a Scientific Information Platform*, pages 15–23. Springer Berlin Heidelberg, 2013.

Donald Kossmann, Tim Kraska, and Simon Loesing. An evaluation of alternative architectures for transaction processing in the cloud. In *Proceedings of the 2010 ACM SIGMOD International Conference on Management of data*, pages 579–590. ACM, 2010.

Sokol Kosta, Andrius Aucinas, Pan Hui, Richard Mortier, and Xinwen Zhang. Unleashing the power of mobile cloud computing using thinkair. *arXiv preprint arXiv:1105.3232*, 2011.

Tim Kraska, Ameet Talwalkar, John C Duchi, Rean Griffith, Michael J Franklin, and Michael I Jordan. Mlbase: A distributed machine-learning system. In *CIDR*, volume 1, pages 2–1, 2013.

Jay Kreps. Questioning the lambda architecture. URL http://radar.oreilly.com/2014/07/questioning-the-lambda-architecture.html.

Mads Daro Kristensen. Scavenger: Transparent development of efficient cyber foraging applications. In *Pervasive Computing and Communications (PerCom), 2010 IEEE International Conference on*, pages 217–226. IEEE, 2010.

Bridget M Kuehn. 1000 genomes project promises closer look at variation in human genome. *Jama*, 300(23):2715–2715, 2008.

Anil Kurmus, Moitrayee Gupta, Roman Pletka, Christian Cachin, and Robert Haas. A comparison of secure multi-tenancy architectures for filesystem storage clouds. In *ACM/IFIP/USENIX International Conference on Distributed Systems Platforms and Open Distributed Processing*, pages 471–490. Springer, 2011.

Guoming Lai, Cuihong Li, Katia Sycara, and Joseph Giampapa. Literature review on multi-attribute negotiations. *Robotics Inst., Carnegie Mellon Univ., Pittsburgh, PA, Tech. Rep. CMU-RI-TR-04-66*, 2004.

Edward A Lee. Cyber-physical systems-are computing foundations adequate. In *Position paper for NSF workshop on cyber-physical systems: research motivation, techniques and roadmap*, volume 2, pages 1–9. Citeseer, 2006.

Jay Lee, Behrad Bagheri, and Hung-An Kao. A cyber-physical systems architecture for industry 4.0-based manufacturing systems. *Manufacturing letters*, 3:18–23, 2015.

ZhenJiang Li, Cheng Chen, and Kai Wang. Cloud computing for agent-based urban transportation systems. *IEEE Intelligent Systems*, 26(1):73–79, 2011.

Jimmy Lin and Alek Kolcz. Large-scale machine learning at twitter. In *Proceedings of the 2012 ACM SIGMOD International Conference on Management of Data*, pages 793–804. ACM, 2012.

Jimmy Lin and Dmitriy Ryaboy. Scaling big data mining infrastructure: the twitter experience. *ACM SIGKDD Explorations Newsletter*, 14(2):6–19, 2013.

Bin Liu, Shu Gui Cao, and Wu He. Distributed data mining for e-business. *Information Technology and Management*, 12(2):67–79, 2011.

Juan Liu, Yuyi Mao, Jun Zhang, and Khaled B Letaief. Delay-optimal computation task scheduling for mobile-edge computing systems. In *2016 IEEE International Symposium on Information Theory (ISIT)*, pages 1451–1455. IEEE, 2016.

Tomás Sánchez López, Alexandra Brintrup, Marc-André Isenberg, and Jeanette Mansfeld. Resource management in the internet of things: Clustering, synchronisation and software agents. In *Architecting the Internet of Things*, pages 159–193. Springer, 2011.

Yucheng Low, Joseph E Gonzalez, Aapo Kyrola, Danny Bickson, Carlos E Guestrin, and Joseph Hellerstein. Graphlab: A new framework for parallel machine learning. *arXiv preprint arXiv:1408.2041*, 2014.

Pavel Mach and Zdenek Becvar. Mobile edge computing: A survey on architecture and computation offloading. *IEEE Communications Surveys & Tutorials*, 19(3):1628–1656, 2017.

Zaigham Mahmood and Richard Hill. *Cloud Computing for enterprise architectures*. Springer Science & Business Media, 2011.

Grzegorz Malewicz, Matthew H Austern, Aart JC Bik, James C Dehnert, Ilan Horn, Naty Leiser, and Grzegorz Czajkowski. Pregel: a system for large-scale graph processing. In *Proceedings of the 2010 ACM SIGMOD International Conference on Management of data*, pages 135–146. ACM, 2010.

Matthew Malloy, Paul Barford, Enis Ceyhun Alp, Jonathan Koller, and Adria Jewell. Internet device graphs. In *Proceedings of the 23rd ACM SIGKDD International Conference on Knowledge Discovery and Data Mining*, pages 1913–1921. ACM, 2017.

James Manyika. Big data: The next frontier for innovation, competition, and productivity. *http://www.mckinsey.com/Insights/MGI/Research/Technology_and_Innovation/Big_data_The_next_frontier_for_innovation*, 2011.

Verdi March, Yan Gu, Erwin Leonardi, George Goh, Markus Kirchberg, and
Bu Sung Lee. μcloud: towards a new paradigm of rich mobile applications.
Procedia Computer Science, 5:618–624, 2011.

Nathan Marz. How to beat the cap theorem, 2011. URL http://nathanmarz
.com/blog/how-to-beat-the-cap-theorem.html.

Nathan Marz and James Warren. *Big Data: Principles and best practices of scalable
real-time data systems*. New York; Manning Publications Co., 2015.

Xiangrui Meng, Joseph Bradley, Burak Yavuz, Evan Sparks, Shivaram
Venkataraman, Davies Liu, Jeremy Freeman, DB Tsai, Manish Amde,
Sean Owen, et al. Mllib: Machine learning in apache spark. *The Journal
of Machine Learning Research*, 17(1):1235–1241, 2016.

Gilad Mishne, Jeff Dalton, Zhenghua Li, Aneesh Sharma, and Jimmy Lin.
Fast data in the era of big data: Twitter's real-time related query sugges-
tion architecture. In *Proceedings of the 2013 ACM SIGMOD International
Conference on Management of Data*, pages 1147–1158. ACM, 2013.

Sudip Misra, Snigdha Das, Manas Khatua, and Mohammad S Obaidat.
Qos-guaranteed bandwidth shifting and redistribution in mobile cloud
environment. *IEEE Transactions on Cloud Computing*, 2(2):181–193, 2013.

M Victoria Moreno, Luc Dufour, Antonio F Skarmeta, Antonio J Jara,
Dominique Genoud, Bruno Ladevie, and Jean-Jacques Bezian. Big
data: the key to energy efficiency in smart buildings. *Soft Computing*,
20(5):1749–1762, 2016.

Christopher Moretti, Jared Bulosan, Douglas Thain, and Patrick J Flynn.
All-pairs: An abstraction for data-intensive cloud computing. In *Parallel
and Distributed Processing, 2008. IPDPS 2008. IEEE International Symposium on*, pages 1–11. IEEE, 2008.

D Mourtzis, E Vlachou, and N Milas. Industrial big data as a result of iot
adoption in manufacturing. *Procedia cirp*, 55:290–295, 2016.

Olga Munoz, Antonio Pascual-Iserte, and Josep Vidal. Optimization of radio
and computational resources for energy efficiency in latency-constrained
application offloading. *IEEE Transactions on Vehicular Technology*, 64(10):
4738–4755, 2014.

NASA. Landsat case studies 2018, 2018. URL https://landsat.gsfc.nasa.gov/
wp-content/uploads/2019/02/Case_Studies_Book2018_Landsat_Final_
12x9web.pdf.

Leonardo Neumeyer, Bruce Robbins, Anish Nair, and Anand Kesari. S4:
Distributed stream computing platform. In *Data Mining Workshops
(ICDMW), 2010 IEEE International Conference on*, pages 170–177. IEEE,
2010.

Sam Newman. Building microservices: designing fine-grained systems. 2015.

Maximilian Nickel, Kevin Murphy, Volker Tresp, and Evgeniy Gabrilovich.
A review of relational machine learning for knowledge graphs: From

multi-relational link prediction to automated knowledge graph construction. *arXiv preprint arXiv:1503.00759*, 2015.

Raz Nissim, Ronen I Brafman, and Carmel Domshlak. A general, fully distributed multi-agent planning algorithm. In *Proceedings of the 9th International Conference on Autonomous Agents and Multiagent Systems: volume 1-Volume 1*, pages 1323–1330. International Foundation for Autonomous Agents and Multiagent Systems, 2010.

Amy Nordrum. Popular internet of things forecast of 50 billion devices by 2020 is outdated (2016). *Dosegljivo: https://spectrum. ieee. org/tech-talk/ telecom/internet/popular-internet-ofthings-forecast-of-50-billion-devices-by-2020-is-outdated.[Dostopano: 11. 8. 2017]*, 2017.

Jeffrey M. O'Brien. The race to create a 'smart' google, 2006. URL https://money.cnn.com/magazines/fortune/fortune_archive/2006/11/ 27/8394347/index.htm.

OMG. Cloud customer architecture for mobile. *https://www.omg.org/cloud/ deliverables/cloud-customer-architecture-for-mobile.htm*, 2015.

Brian O'Neill. Delta architectures: Unifying the lambda architecture and leveraging storm from hadoop/rest. URL https://dzone.com/articles/ delta-architectures-unifying.

Benyoucef Othmane and Rahal Sidi Ahmed Hebri. Cloud computing & multi-agent systems: a new promising approach for distributed data mining. In *Information Technology Interfaces (ITI), Proceedings of the ITI 2012 34th International Conference on*, pages 111–116. IEEE, 2012.

Pekka Pääkkönen and Daniel Pakkala. Reference architecture and classification of technologies, products and services for big data systems. *Big Data Research*, 2(4):166–186, 2015.

M P Papazoglou. Service-oriented computing: Concepts, characteristics and directions. In *Web Information Systems Engineering, 2003. WISE 2003. Proceedings of the Fourth International Conference on*, pages 3–12. IEEE, 2003.

Norman W Paton and Oscar Díaz. Active database systems. *ACM Computing Surveys (CSUR)*, 31(1):63–103, 1999.

João Pedro, João Pires, and Joao Paulo Carvalho. Distributed routing path optimization for obs networks based on ant colony optimization. In *Global Telecommunications Conference, 2009. GLOBECOM 2009. IEEE*, pages 1–7. IEEE, 2009.

Matt Pharr and Randima Fernando. *Gpu gems 2: programming techniques for high-performance graphics and general-purpose computation*. Addison-Wesley Professional, 2005.

Jay Pujara, Hui Miao, Lise Getoor, and William Cohen. Knowledge graph identification. In *The Semantic Web–ISWC 2013*, pages 542–557. Springer, 2013.

Elie Raad, Richard Chbeir, and Albert Dipanda. User profile matching in social networks. In *Network-Based Information Systems (NBiS), 2010 13th International Conference on*, pages 297–304. IEEE, 2010.

Anand S Rao and Michael P Georgeff. Modeling rational agents within a bdi-architecture. *KR*, 91:473–484, 1991.

Bhoopathi Rapolu. Internet of aircraft things: An industry set to be transformed. *https://aviationweek.com/connected-aerospace/internet-aircraft-things -industry-set-be-transformed*, 2016.

Ju Ren, Hui Guo, Chugui Xu, and Yaoxue Zhang. Serving at the edge: A scalable iot architecture based on transparent computing. *IEEE Network*, 31 (5):96–105, 2017.

A Rotem-Gal-Oz, E Bruno, and U Dahan. *SOA Patterns*. Manning Publications Co, 2012.

Dominik Ryżko and Aleksander Ihnatowicz. Multi-agent approach to monitoring of systems in soa architecture. In *New Challenges for Intelligent Information and Database Systems*, pages 309–318, 2011.

Dominik Ryżko and Henryk Rybiński. Distributed default logic for multi-agent system. In *2006 IEEE/WIC/ACM International Conference on Intelligent Agent Technology*, pages 204–210. IEEE, 2006.

Dominik Ryżko, Henryk Rybiński, and Przemyslaw Wiech. Learning mechanism for distributed default logic based mas-implementation considerations. In *Proceedings of the International IIS 2008 Conference*, pages 329–338, 2008.

Ichiro Satoh. Dynamic deployment of pervasive services. In *Pervasive Services, 2005. ICPS'05. Proceedings. International Conference on*, pages 302–311. IEEE, 2005.

Mahadev Satyanarayanan. The emergence of edge computing. *Computer*, 50 (1):30–39, 2017.

Mahadev Satyanarayanan, Paramvir Bahl, Ramón Caceres, and Nigel Davies. The case for vm-based cloudlets in mobile computing. *IEEE pervasive Computing*, (4):14–23, 2009.

Ben Schmaus, Chris Carey, Neeraj Joshi, Nick Mahilani, and Sharma Podila. Stream-processing with mantis, 2016. URL http://techblog.netflix.com/ 2016/03/stream-processing-with-mantis.html.

Ingrid Scholl, Til Aach, Thomas M Deserno, and Torsten Kuhlen. Challenges of medical image processing. *Computer science-Research and development*, 26(1-2):5–13, 2011.

John R Searle and John Rogers Searle. *Speech acts: An essay in the philosophy of language*, volume 626. Cambridge University Press, 1969.

Weiming Shen, Qi Hao, Hyun Joong Yoon, and Douglas H Norrie. Applications of agent-based systems in intelligent manufacturing: An updated review. *Advanced engineering INFORMATICS*, 20(4):415–431, 2006.

Umar Siddiqui, Ghalib Ahmed Tahir, Attiq Ur Rehman, Zahra Ali, Raihan Ur Rasool, and Peter Bloodsworth. Elastic jade: Dynamically scalable multi agents using cloud resources. In *2012 Second International Conference on Cloud and Green Computing*, pages 167–172. IEEE, 2012.

Yogesh Simmhan, Saima Aman, Alok Kumbhare, Rongyang Liu, Sam Stevens, Qunzhi Zhou, and Viktor Prasanna. Cloud-based software platform for big data analytics in smart grids. *Computing in Science & Engineering*, 15(4): 38–47, 2013.

Aarti Singh, Dimple Juneja, and Manisha Malhotra. Autonomous agent based load balancing algorithm in cloud computing. *Procedia Computer Science*, 45:832–841, 2015.

Kamaldeep Singh, Sharath Chandra Guntuku, Abhishek Thakur, and Chittaranjan Hota. Big data analytics framework for peer-to-peer botnet detection using random forests. *Information Sciences*, 278:488–497, 2014.

Amit Singhal. Introducing the knowledge graph: things, not strings. *Official Google Blog, May*, 2012.

Volker Springel, Simon D. M. White, Adrian Jenkins, Carlos S. Frenk, Naoki Yoshida, Liang Gao, Julio Navarro, Robert Thacker, Darren Croton, John Helly, John A. Peacock, Shaun Cole, Peter Thomas, Hugh Couchman, August Evrard, Jörg Colberg, and Frazer Pearce. Simulations of the formation, evolution and clustering of galaxies and quasars. *Nature*, 435:629–636, 2005.

Jaideep Srivastava, Robert Cooley, Mukund Deshpande, and Pang-Ning Tan. Web usage mining: Discovery and applications of usage patterns from web data. *Acm Sigkdd Explorations Newsletter*, 1(2):12–23, 2000.

Statistica.com. Most popular social networks worldwide as of january 2018. URL https://www.statista.com/statistics/272014/global-social-networks-ranked-by-number-of-users/.

Zachary D Stephens, Skylar Y Lee, Faraz Faghri, Roy H Campbell, Chengxiang Zhai, Miles J Efron, Ravishankar Iyer, Michael C Schatz, Saurabh Sinha, and Gene E Robinson. Big data: astronomical or genomical? *PLoS biology*, 13(7): e1002195, 2015.

John E Stone, David Gohara, and Guochun Shi. Opencl: A parallel programming standard for heterogeneous computing systems. *Computing in science & engineering*, 12(3):66, 2010.

Michael Stonebraker, Uğur Çetintemel, and Stan Zdonik. The 8 requirements of real-time stream processing. *SIGMOD Rec.*, 34(4):42–47, December 2005. ISSN 0163-5808. doi: 10.1145/1107499.1107504. URL http://doi.acm.org/10.1145/1107499.1107504.

Yu Su, Shengqi Yang, Huan Sun, Mudhakar Srivatsa, Sue Kase, Michelle Vanni, and Xifeng Yan. Exploiting relevance feedback in knowledge graph search. In *Proceedings of the 21th ACM SIGKDD International*

Conference on Knowledge Discovery and Data Mining, pages 1135–1144. ACM, 2015.

George Suciu, Alexandru Vulpe, Simona Halunga, Octavian Fratu, Gyorgy Todoran, and Victor Suciu. Smart cities built on resilient cloud computing and secure internet of things. In *2013 19th International Conference on Control Systems and Computer Science*, pages 513–518. IEEE, 2013.

Summingbird. Summingbird - github repository. URL https://github.com/twitter/summingbird.

Jorg Swetina, Guang Lu, Philip Jacobs, Francois Ennesser, and JaeSeung Song. Toward a standardized common m2m service layer platform: Introduction to onem2m. *IEEE Wireless Communications*, 21(3):20–26, 2014.

Domenico Talia. Toward cloud-based big-data analytics. *IEEE Computer Science*, pages 98–101, 2013.

Nam Khanh Tran. Classification and learning-to-rank approaches for cross-device matching at cikm cup 2016. *arXiv preprint arXiv:1612.07117*, 2016.

Chi-Ho Tsang and Sam Kwong. Multi-agent intrusion detection system in industrial network using ant colony clustering approach and unsupervised feature extraction. In *2005 IEEE international conference on industrial technology*, pages 51–56. IEEE, 2005.

Zeynep Tufekci. Big questions for social media big data: Representativeness, validity and other methodological pitfalls. *ICWSM*, 14:505–514, 2014.

Bartłomiej Twardowski and Dominik Ryżko. Multi-agent architecture for real-time big data processing. In *Web Intelligence (WI) and Intelligent Agent Technologies (IAT), 2014 IEEE/WIC/ACM International Joint Conferences on*, volume 3, pages 333–337, Aug 2014. 10.1109/WI-IAT.2014.185.

Bartłomiej Twardowski and Dominik Ryżko. Iot and context-aware mobile recommendations using multi-agent systems. In *2015 IEEE/WIC/ACM International Conference on Web Intelligence and Intelligent Agent Technology (WI-IAT)*, volume 1, pages 33–40. IEEE, 2015.

Leslie G Valiant. A bridging model for parallel computation. *Communications of the ACM*, 33(8):103–111, 1990.

W3C. Linking open data. URL http://esw.w3.org/topic/SweoIG/TaskForces/CommunityProjects/LinkingOpenData.

Jun Wang, Weinan Zhang, Shuai Yuan, et al. Display advertising with real-time bidding (rtb) and behavioural targeting. *Foundations and Trends® in Information Retrieval*, 11(4-5):297–435, 2017a.

Peng Wang, Dan Meng, Jizhong Han, Jianfeng Zhan, Bibo Tu, Xiaofeng Shi, and Le Wan. Transformer: a new paradigm for building data-parallel programming models. *IEEE micro*, (4):55–64, 2010.

Shiyong Wang, Jiafu Wan, Di Li, and Chunhua Zhang. Implementing smart factory of industrie 4.0: an outlook. *International Journal of Distributed Sensor Networks*, 12(1):3159805, 2016.

Wanyuan Wang, Yichuan Jiang, and Weiwei Wu. Multiagent-based resource allocation for energy minimization in cloud computing systems. *IEEE Transactions on Systems, Man, and Cybernetics: Systems*, 47(2):205–220, 2017b.

Sage A Weil, Scott A Brandt, Ethan L Miller, and Carlos Maltzahn. Crush: Controlled, scalable, decentralized placement of replicated data. In *SC'06: Proceedings of the 2006 ACM/IEEE Conference on Supercomputing*, pages 31–31. IEEE, 2006.

Sage A Weil, Andrew W Leung, Scott A Brandt, and Carlos Maltzahn. Rados: a scalable, reliable storage service for petabyte-scale storage clusters. In *Proceedings of the 2nd international workshop on Petascale data storage: held in conjunction with Supercomputing'07*, pages 35–44. ACM, 2007.

Gerhard Weiss. *Multiagent systems: a modern approach to distributed artificial intelligence*. MIT press, 1999.

Andrew Whitmore, Anurag Agarwal, and Li Da Xu. The internet of things-a survey of topics and trends. *Information Systems Frontiers*, 17(2):261–274, 2015.

Przemyslaw Wiech, Henryk Rybiński, and Dominik Ryżko. Ddld-based reasoning for mas. In *International Symposium on Methodologies for Intelligent Systems*, pages 182–191. Springer, 2011.

Wikipedia. Epcis. URL http://en.wikipedia.org/wiki/EPCglobal.

Stephen Witt. Data management and analytics for utilities 2014, 2014. URL https://assets.fiercemarkets.net/public/sites/energy/reports/bdasmartgridreport.pdf.

Jiyan Wu, Chau Yuen, Ngai-Man Cheung, Junliang Chen, and Chang Wen Chen. Enabling adaptive high-frame-rate video streaming in mobile cloud gaming applications. *IEEE Transactions on Circuits and Systems for Video Technology*, 25(12):1988–2001, 2015.

Kun-Lung Wu, Kirsten W Hildrum, Wei Fan, Philip S Yu, Charu C Aggarwal, David A George, Buğra Gedik, Eric Bouillet, Xiaohui Gu, Gang Luo, et al. Challenges and experience in prototyping a multi-modal stream analytic and monitoring application on system s. In *Proceedings of the 33rd international conference on Very large data bases*, pages 1185–1196. VLDB Endowment, 2007.

Miao Wu, Ting-Jie Lu, Fei-Yang Ling, Jing Sun, and Hui-Ying Du. Research on the architecture of internet of things. In *2010 3rd International Conference on Advanced Computer Theory and Engineering (ICACTE)*, volume 5, pages V5–484. IEEE, 2010.

Zhiang Wu, Jie Cao, and Changjian Fang. Data cloud for distributed data mining via pipelined mapreduce. In *International Workshop on Agents and Data Mining Interaction*, pages 316–330. Springer, 2011.

Oliver Wyman. Mro survey 2016 aviation, mro big data – a lion or a lamb? innovation and adoption in aviation mro, 2016. URL http://www .oliverwyman.com/our-expertise/insights/2016/apr/mro-survey-2016 .html.

Reynold S Xin, Josh Rosen, Matei Zaharia, Michael J Franklin, Scott Shenker, and Ion Stoica. Shark: Sql and rich analytics at scale. In *Proceedings of the 2013 ACM SIGMOD International Conference on Management of data*, pages 13–24. ACM, 2013.

Xiaomin Xu, Sheng Huang, Yaoliang Chen, Kevin Browny, Inge Halilovicy, and Wei Lu. Tsaaas: Time series analytics as a service on iot. In *2014 IEEE International Conference on Web Services*, pages 249–256. IEEE, 2014.

Hung-chih Yang, Ali Dasdan, Ruey-Lung Hsiao, and D Stott Parker. Map-reduce-merge: simplified relational data processing on large clusters. In *Proceedings of the 2007 ACM SIGMOD international conference on Management of data*, pages 1029–1040. ACM, 2007.

Chengqi Zhang, Zili Zhang, and Longbing Cao. Agents and data mining: Mutual enhancement by integration. In *International Workshop on Autonomous Intelligent Systems: Agents and Data Mining*, pages 50–61. Springer, 2005.

Yaoxue Zhang and Yuezhi Zhou. Transparent computing: Spatio-temporal extension on von neumann architecture for cloud services. *Tsinghua Science and Technology*, 18(1):10–21, 2013.

Zehua Zhang and Xuejie Zhang. Realization of open cloud computing federation based on mobile agent. In *Intelligent Computing and Intelligent Systems, 2009. ICIS 2009. IEEE International Conference on*, volume 3, pages 642–646. IEEE, 2009.

Zhao Zhang, Kyle Barbary, Frank Austin Nothaft, Evan Sparks, Oliver Zahn, Michael J Franklin, David A Patterson, and Saul Perlmutter. Scientific computing meets big data technology: An astronomy use case. In *Big Data (Big Data), 2015 IEEE International Conference on*, pages 918–927. IEEE, 2015.

Kaile Zhou, Chao Fu, and Shanlin Yang. Big data driven smart energy management: From big data to big insights. *Renewable and Sustainable Energy Reviews*, 56:215–225, 2016.

Yunyue Zhu and Dennis Shasha. Statstream: Statistical monitoring of thousands of data streams in real time. In *Proceedings of the 28th International Conference on Very Large Data Bases*, VLDB '02, pages 358–369. VLDB Endowment, 2002. URL http://dl.acm.org/citation.cfm?id=1287369 .1287401.

INDEX